INTI

Do you love yourself enough to love someone else? Come explore the inner woman, with author Terry Smith, as she takes us on the campaign trail to gain back our sense of "self" and personal harmony. Experience the freedom that can result from speaking your mind when *you* need to, and accepting the results of the decisions *we* choose to make.

Smith uses rich life experience to show women how to focus their energies on loving themselves first, before seeking love elsewhere. Every reader will be taken on a tour de force of man-woman relationships, and why they often fail before having a chance to succeed.

Explore how you too, can take command of your choices and destiny, by removing all doubts and insecurities with the discipline of intimacy and communication. Nobody knows your self, better than you. Learn more about the "real" you, before offering up that person in a relationship with someone else.

"Teaching the Discipline of Intimacy and Communication", will take you inside yourself for a journey that could change your life!

Teaching the D.I.C.

Discipline of Intimacy and Communication

Freedom Comes With Taking Ownership of Your Choices

First Press Direct, Inc.

PUBLISHED BY FIRST PRESS DIRECT, INC.
www.firstpressdirect.com
First Press Direct, Inc.
2778 Cumberland Blvd, #233
Smyrna, GA 30080

First Edition

**The Library of Congress catalog Card No.: 2002115640
ISBN: 0-9724016-8-7**

Cover design by Sami Bentil
Illustration design by Sami Bentil
Graphic design by William "Jay" Jackson III
Edited by Betty Sleep
Layout design by Wendy Lamirande

Teaching the D.I.C.

Discipline of Intimacy and Communication

freedom comes with

taking ownership of

your choices

TERRY SMITH

Dedication

My gratitude always:

Mom & Dad: thank you for instilling in me individuality and a sense of independence. Grace, you have redefined the image of a stepmother. Your word and your love have been my rocks. My sisters, Cheryl and Jakki: thank you for all the encouragement, limitless support and for insisting that your sister's dream come true. My brothers: Richard as the first-born and my big brother, an enormous amount of expectations fell upon you. I am proud to say that you have surpassed them all and there is no doubt that your first-born Cory will call you his mentor. Michael, it is only fitting that my baby brother grows up to be larger than me. You have always ensured that all your sisters were loved equally. Timothy: you're my favorite brother-n-law. James: you have a wonderful spirit and a gentle personality. Thanks for being Mom's best friend, lover and soulmate – welcome to the family.

Karen Freeman, Tanya Dingle and Sandra Johnson, we've been together for so long that we'd make credible sources for the Enquirer. I love you!

My real women girlfriends: Thanks for not removing my name from the "Girls Night Out" guest list, even though I'm known for RSVPing that I will be there and canceling out for a date with a man. That you continue to invite me shows our bond is strong and our love for one another eternal, or is it simply that you all remember what I told you "with a man I don't have to pull out my wallet. Call you later."... *(wink)*

All of my BOA Cheerleaders. You know who you are!

Acknowledgements

Sami Bentil: When the phone rang I could not believe it was renowned Artist, Sami Bentil on the other end. He heard about an unknown author (with no money) looking for someone to design her book cover. Knowing this, he still called. He introduced himself and proceeded to modestly give his credentials and his gracious reason for calling. I thought, no need for modesty. I was familiar with his works "Maskitos" on the set of "Living Single", "Go Forth and Be Fruitful" as well as his name and I said, " I can't pay you, your worth". He laughed and said it would be his honor to design a piece of original artwork for my book. Bless you Sami.

Betty Sleep: for demanding only the best writing from me and not accepting anything less. Now that it's over I can really tell you how I feel. You're a perfectionist, you work late, you're always reliable, you added polish to my manuscript. Personally, I think you are just too caring of others' projects and for that I am proud that you will work with me.

E. Earle Burke: my attorney and good friend, we stand together as one.

Dr. Harold Jackson, as well as all of the wonderful men whose shoulders never tired from my leaning on them for advice and support. Thank you for exemplifying God's meaning of a good man.

Thank you for your generosity: Rachel Jamerson, of Rachel's Island and Island Cruises & Tours, Rudell Richardson, South Consulting, Inc., Calvin Moody, of State Farms Insurance, Kevin Jackson, William Jackson, of Platinum Plus Graphics, Tkeban Jahannes, of Image Matters, Todd A. Smith, of Hairston's Dinner Club

To:

My earthly angel
Tammie McGowan, you are my conscience
Thank you for believing in me…

EXALT

To: God

You have given me your words of comfort, love that's unconditional, endless, and incomparable. You see my heart like no other because when you stood at the door I welcomed you in. You came with all your gracious gifts of good news, love, forgiveness and your promises to never leave or forsake me. You over flowed my heart so that I have a limitless amount of love to give to others. There is much I will never know, but I do know that I am one of the many that you have prepared a place for. Your wisdom is boundless, and your love unduplicated.

Thank you to my parents for your obedience. When I was a child I came to you for comfort; now that I am an adult I know that I can go to Matthew 6:9-15.

I Surrender All

Dedication...

Lillian R.C. Smith
Dora A. Moore
Grace M. Sheppard

CONTENTS

"I Am Perfect"

I have been asked countless times, how I learned to speak and walk with such confidence. My answer is the same every time—my Mother. Mother shared with me, some memorable words of wisdom, right after she found the strength to overcome an enormous personal barrier—abandonment, the feeling of incompetence, and the fear to trust in her will. Mother had allowed this mountain to block her view of the possibilities that were before her.

The moral lessons my Mother conveyed in every day life, often reminded me of the old gray-haired lady on the pages of books I checked out of the library. The beginning of many stories I read, had an inquisitive little boy who stumbled across a weathered porch on which sat a non-expressive old woman. In the middle of the story the old woman shares with the boy words of wisdom, fables, or advice that he clearly can't understand at the time. The artwork on the next page shows a close-up of his face appearing confused. By the end of the story he comes to appreciate those words, and the old woman is pleased that he has arrived at this understanding, so that her teaching did not fall on deaf ears.

Today, I would describe my Mother as a woman who had the strength to endure rejection and humiliation from society, friends, and even family. She reached inside herself and drew on that strength, giving her the will to keep moving forward.

My Mother emphasized the importance of loving myself and finding the power within me. That was my will, and I should never give it up to anyone else. I remember clearly, when she shared those insightful lessons, she would look intently into my eyes and say, "You are perfect, just the way you are." This taught me that I *am* perfect as myself! She often stressed that no one is better at being the person I am than me, and that's why I should become the best me that I can. Thanks to her gentle words of encouragement, I found the courage to do just that.

My Mother gave me many words of wisdom even when I was quite young. I would say "Mommy, I'm being nice", trying to impress her. She would reply, "It is better to be kind than nice. Being *nice* is politically correct: you are *supposed* to be nice, but *kindness* is a choice." Those are powerful words to say to a young person, and they came from a woman who did not find her personal power, until well into adulthood.

There is one vivid memory—no, let's call it a "meeting of the minds" —I have of Mother. It took place when she was going through the most depressing part of her divorce from my father.

My parents' marriage, you might say, started prematurely. My Mother was seventeen years old, pregnant and under the legal age, so when she married Father, he became her legal guardian. Until then, Mother had never traveled out of her hometown.

Father was in the Navy and absent for most of our childhoods. Within a few months of the marriage, this once-sheltered girl who had been intimate with a man she loved unconditionally, was on her own and expecting a child. Throughout Mother's pregnancy Father emphasized his want, desire and wishes to have a baby girl. Feeling like a failure,

Mother was thrust into the lonely bowels of military motherhood with her nine-pound baby boy.

It was no surprise to my Mother that my father really wanted a girl, so as usual, she was willing to comply. Within three years she gave him two daughters—first myself, and then my sister.

Marriage to a military man was frightening and challenging, but worst of all lonely, especially for someone who had never even crossed the State line. Father was a world-traveler and accustomed to moving around. Mother, on the other hand was not. Looking back, I don't think that Father had any empathy for his wife's predicament, but neither did most 1960s military men. Those were the years of the Vietnam wars. Military life wasn't quite what it is today. The expectations of a military wife, were much like the closing words of an old black-and-white movie I saw many years ago: "take it like a soldier's wife ought".

The life was hard on my Mother, her troubles seeming magnified by the distance between her and her own Mother. Even though their relationship had always been strained, Grandmother was really the only other person my Mother had any interaction with on her side of the family.

Father wasn't around to help much, but when he was present, he had duties outside of the home, and my Mother was still left with the chores of caring for her home, husband and children.

I'm not saying my father was a terrible dictator who never cared about my Mother. He did try in his own way. When he was home, he would teach her how to shop, balance a checkbook, and drive a car, but even while teaching, he criticized her if she had trouble doing things that he thought were only common sense. A little constructive criticism is good for the soul, but too much negative criticism can break a spirit if it is allowed to continue. Maybe Mother heard enough good "buts" to convince herself that everything was alright... "*but* he always tells me how nice the kids look, *but* he said the house looks nice, *but* he really liked the dinner that I cooked for him," *but, but, but.* I have a but: But did he like the way you stood up for yourself when you needed to?

I was twelve years old, my sister was eleven, and my brother was fourteen, when my parents' marriage ended.

The evening my Mother called me into her bedroom was the same day she stood in the middle of the den and announced she and my father had divorced. The look on her face is one that I'll never forget. It was devoid of emotion, her skin pale and bloodless, her eyes staring but seeing nothing. She turned and went immediately to her room, slowly shutting the door behind her.

The mood during the rest of the day was quiet and somber. Only whispered voices and empathy for my Mother, between my brother and sister, to one another. Divorced... I was sitting alone, unable to believe that my daddy would leave me, unless Mother did something to make him go. As daddy's first daughter, it was no secret that I was his favorite and he was my favorite parent. I expected Mother to call my brother or sister— one of her favorites—into her room. They were the ones she always seemed to gravitate toward when she needed someone's support. This is why I was surprised to find she wanted me.

I was definitely not my Mother's favorite, yet I was the one whom she called into her room. It was a small, boxlike room, dim with brownish-orange shadows coming from a single lamp that sat next to her bed. The light barely touched the corner of the room in which my Mother's bed sat. It was an almost lifeless atmosphere, as if someone was giving up on everything.

I slipped between the door and its frame, letting a few seconds pass before my eyes adjusted to the light in the room. I called to her so she would recognize in my voice, that she had selected the wrong child. "Yes, ma'am, you called me," I said in a whisper. She beckoned me to her. I reached for a light switch on the wall next to the door. "Don't turn on the light," she said in a faint mumble. "Come over here and sit on the bed." I hadn't seen my Mother since she'd said that my daddy had left me.

Today I know that my father only left my Mother, but back then I was a daddy's girl, and only thinking of myself. I moved toward Mother's bed, curious yet disgusted as I gazed at her. My steps were careful and short. I was trying to rationalize why my Mother looked so strange. Her eyes were puffy, her hair was a mess, and she was still wearing the same clothes from the day before. Twisted and wet tissues were on the floor next to her bed and nightstand.

Now that I was beside her, I could see that she had been crying. I started to sit at the foot of her bed, but just as I had shifted my weight she said, "Come closer." Once I could see her sorrow up close, I was afraid. I felt that if I came a little closer I would start crying, too. "Come closer," she repeated. I moved closer, but unwillingly.

She grabbed both of my hands and said, "You are going to grow up one day and find a husband. Don't let what happened to me happen to you. I did everything that your father asked of me, even if I didn't want to. I never faltered. I moved every time your father said move. This time I didn't want to, because I wanted to keep you kids in school. He left me down here in the South, worlds away from my family. I believe there's another woman. He's always had reasons that sounded like excuses as to why he stopped coming home as much on the weekends. Your father isn't a kind person. He can be nice, but he's not kind."

She drew my arms toward her as she said "Listen to me, Terry. Be certain of what you expect in a relationship with a man. Know your self-worth." I felt her hands tighten around my adolescent arms. "Intimacy is impossible without communication. Find that power within you that gives you the strength to convey your expectations, needs, and wants in a relationship. Don't lose yourself and act on someone else's power. It is more important to like someone than to love." The squeezing was becoming unbearable. I thought I was going to cry.

"You will find that if you really like them, you will love liking them. When you find someone with whom you want to spend your life, let the decision be made by your will. Right now, I don't even know who I am or what I want. Be with someone because it feels right to you, not because it feels right to him.

First, take the time to feel the difference. My Mother never pre-pared me for life, and I am not going to do that to you."

I understood what she meant, or at least I thought I did. At that time all I could think about was that she was hurting my arm. When I looked down, she'd released her hold. The skin where she had gripped me was turning a deep maroon.

At the time of the divorce, my Mother was in her early thirties. She had been very submissive during her marriage, catering to all of my father's needs or directives.

When I tell the story of how my Mother announced to my siblings and me that she and my father were divorced—not separated, but divorced, people anticipate more drama to the story. Yet it happened very simply, and without any warning. There was nothing in our abode that appeared to be unbalanced. Everything appeared normal. Now, looking back, I can see why I was so clueless. My father traveled most of my childhood, so if there was a separation period, my siblings and I -were unaware of it.

My Mother continued without my father, taking care of her family, home, and herself even when she felt the world was against her. It was difficult in the beginning, learning to trust in her self. It would be a long time before she was secure in expressing how she felt, accepting that what she knew inside, she was allowed to say. Because of her love for others, she was willing and determined to change. I know now why she chose to speak to me and not the favorite children. She knew that I would be the most affected by my father's absence and in a way, it was her start to making key D.I.C. changes in her life.

Today my Mother has triumphed. She is self-assured, confident, and certain of herself. She is married to her best friend and she is amazingly happy.

Children are like sponges, they absorb everything. Remember, there is power in the words you say to your children and to others.

Part I:

So, You Think
You Know Yourself ...

Chapter 1

Preface

I know a woman who speaks with frustration every time she discusses her volatile relationship.

Lust and an explosive atmosphere ignited by lies, mistrust and deceitfulness hold the relationship together. Inevitably, she chooses to quench the fire by demanding an immediate separation period—and equally inevitable, the flame is lit again when he ignores her ban and creates ways to see her.

Part I: So, You Think You Know Yourself...

In fact, it's usually this period of non-communication that actually fuels the passion that they both find in an empty relationship

I admire the confidence he displays both in exhibiting his will and the certainty of her response. The intensity of the relationship heightens his emotions and strengthens his desire to see her. He is confident that if she sees him, he will have her in his arms. And she is also confident—of him. She once told me, "He knows exactly how to touch, stroke and place his hands on every one of my buttons and he won't stop. The passion between us is exhausting. He knows what seeing him does to me".

Clearly, he's not doing anything she's not willing to have done to her, but my friend blames him and that makes her feel helpless and not in control of her choices.

I am going to end this story leaving you wanting more. There is no amusement in a relationship that's volatile, out of control, and has no future.

My friend's story likely sounds familiar to many women. It contains plenty of passion but little real emotion—and therefore lacks satisfaction. Many women are in a passive state of denial, because they take no responsibility for their willingness to participate in unfulfilling relationships.

"Teaching the D.I.C." is an observational perspective of relationships. It is your invitation to a freedom party. The menu selection includes appetizers: alternatives, the main course: communication, and a sweet dessert: intimacy. The only requirement to attend is that you are willing to be truthful and expose the restraints that bind you—restraints such as fear, blame, and guilt.

In order to appreciate what an understanding of D.I.C. can bring, we need to look at life's lessons without the D.I.C. and explore why we, as women, exchange our true desires for denial and grief. What is it that inhibits us from exercising the freedom of our choice? At this party, I encourage you to over-indulge yourself in liberation. Look at, in, and through your self, to see "the real you" as never before.

Who in your life, can truly say that they have an intimate relationship with you? Is it someone that has taken the initiative to apply the D.I.C. to know your fears, dreams, inner thoughts and hopes? Is your mate truly intimate with you and completely communicative—or do you just wish he were? Communication takes more than one person wanting to ask questions—it requires another willing to answer.

Part I: So, You Think You Know Yourself...

Many women avoid familiarity to spite themselves. Some aren't even disciplined enough to ask a man they're seeing, if he is dating anyone else. How often have you dressed for a second date, wondering if it's the right time to ask whether the relationship is exclusive?

In this book, I will share personal stories of life's lessons without the D.I.C. I want women who are feeling pain from a brief relationship that has ended, to take responsibility for their own heartache.

Over the years, I have listened to countless stories of failed relationships, where women say, "I thought. I thought—I thought he loved me, I thought he was straight, I thought he would be there if I got pregnant; I thought, I thought, I thought." In the morning these women are barely able to get out of bed and face themselves in a mirror, after the end of another disappointing relationship. Their wounds never close, they just get bandaged with another temporary relationship, steeped in anger, guilt and a wish that the last one, gets his.

One way not to get wounded in the first place is to change "I thought" to "I know". When you have doubts, just ask. By doing this, you are taking ownership of your choices. Maybe things won't work out the way that you want. But when you take responsibility for your decision, you will at least be able to live with the choices you've made.

I am not a psychologist, but I do have rich life experience. That's why I am writing this book: to share the lessons I've learnt both in my life and from the lives of other women I've known.

Much of our reluctance to question things comes down to fear. Why do some women worry that they will be left alone if they openly communicate their relationship expectations? As a gender, we adhere to the perception that women are passive creatures. Passive is okay, but so is aggression. Being assertive means standing up for what will make you feel good about yourself.

What is the formula men use when they meet a woman, that determines within minutes of the conversation if she would accept a relationship with no commitment? Are men born with a testosterone-fuelled, commitment detector? Is it because women have no testosterone, that they can't see when he just wants sex and no ties? Do some women slip through this commitment radar sweep, because they are afraid to verbalize their expectations at the beginning?

Teaching the D.I.C. presents techniques to develop an intimate relationship with someone and clearly explains the repercussions of saying "no" when you really mean "yes". It explores the feelings that may result from failing to communicate your desires and how to take responsibility for the breakdown. In short, this book discusses ways to communicate effectively. Communication of any sort is good if what has been expressed is understood by the receiver. As the communicator, your objective is to enlighten or to ensure that one understands. When exchanging informative dialogue, phrase your question in a way that will lead to achieving your goal, which is to eliminate the wonder.

We live in a world full of fault and blame, where responsibility is a burden that must be avoided at all costs. By applying a 'must-have' D.I.C. attitude, you can and will, re-gain your freedom of choice. Others may not like what you say, but the honesty will bring you self-respect. This book is not intended to be a comprehensive text that lays out rules on how to fix your life, but it does contain the lessons of a life without D.I.C. As my Mother so wisely states, "Life often gives us the opportunity to make a choice. We must then take responsibility for it—after all, in the end, we're the ones who have to live with the results."

As for me, while employing the teachings in this book, I have experienced gratifying love, grief, and some disappoint-

ments. However, I have learned that through all my past experiences (good, bad or indifferent), each aspect of each relationship was my choice and I feel good about each one.

If one person uses D.I.C. to gain freedom and ultimately
take responsibility for their choices, then the success of this book
is magnified a hundred times. I wrote *Teaching the D.I.C.* for
those women living with a cavity in their life full of denial and
regret, when they don't need to.

Think of a time when you heard someone blurt something
out in a room filled with people. Everyone in the room stops
talking, their faces wearing looks of pseudo-shock. They can't
believe that someone has finally expressed what none of them
had the nerve to say. I've always admired people who have the
guts to speak up. I am just someone who wants you to feel better
about yourself and who wants to help women stop giving the
power to men, by blaming them when they aren't around.

When I decided to write this book, I knew what I wanted
the heart of the book to be. I wanted *Teaching the Discipline of
Intimacy and Communication* to convey how important it is to *like*
someone enough to be able to communicate those sometimes
difficult truths about your relationship. (Remember, it's okay if
you don't love at this time.) I also wanted to help readers deal

with a relationship that they didn't end, and take control of their own choices. In Chapter 3: "I Am Perfect," I share my beautiful Mother's profound words of empowerment, expressing the sanctity of intimacy in its true definition.

It wasn't difficult finding the words contained in this book. Every story and lesson weighed on my heart and in my mind. The greatest difficulty was deciding on a title that would express all the important elements that make up the text as a whole.

Sometimes at the end of a movie there will be clips left on the editing room floor. These scenes didn't make the cut. Similarly, in writing this book, many otherwise relevant sections were left out in favor of material that emphasizes *like* before *love*.

Didn't make the cut:

If You Like Me Today, Will You Love Me Forever?

So You Love Me, but Do You Like Me?

Help! I Realize I Love You, but I Don't Like You

I Never Liked You, So How Can I Love You?

Chapter 2

What is Good D.I.C.?

Good D.I.C is when you are intimately familiar with someone's wants, needs, and desires. The only way to ensure this is
through communication—a productive exchange that enlightens
and builds understanding. You may be giving information that
helps someone better understand your personality, goals and
aspirations, or asking questions to eliminate guessing, gather
facts and engage in meaningful conversation. This is true communication, and the results may help you to feel a sense of comfort in making decisions.

Part I: So, You Think You Know Yourself...

Many people are uncomfortable asking questions. Often, long after the conversation, we find ourselves wishing we had asked something that we chose to leave unspoken. With discipline and practice, you can ask questions in a way that reduces discomfort. Phrasing questions in a way that invites dialogue helps the receiver and you too. Discipline is the presence of mind to maintain your focus no matter what the circumstances might be. By putting into practice good D.I.C., you can stop the wondering, guessing, and misperceptions that develop before a relationship has had a chance.

Odds are, you can find a thousand books emphasizing the importance of *love* in our lives, but there are probably less than a hundred emphasizing the word *like,* which is equally important. This book contains personal stories of relationships without good D.I.C. as well as how to feel better by re-channeling energy used to blame others, into effective decisions you are happy living with. The Communication & Intimacy Techniques outlined in Chapter 23, offer an opportunity to learn and develop effective communication skills, while gaining the clarity essential for all relationships.

Chapter 2, "Why Do We Wonder?" is based on observations and the personal experiences of others. Its primary purpose is to help you find reasons why we choose to wonder, guess, or assume things, rather than ask a question that initiates a give-and-take exchange, eliminating the doubt.

So many of us are frustrated and emotionally distraught over love: absence of love, passion without love, misunderstood affection, or unreciprocated and therefore unfulfilled devotion. From my perspective, self-love is the greatest love of all. No matter who loves you or whom you love, the love of self is a condition that should supersede all.

If you need the adulation of others or feel that you need to be loved by another to love yourself, then you probably are unfulfilled, even if you have yet to admit it. The importance of loving yourself outweighs all other pursuits.

Self-love is essential if you are to receive the love you want and deserve. When you have self-love, you are in tune with what feels good to you, and are a complete person, even without the love of others.

Part I: So, You Think You Know Yourself...

On average, eight out of every ten couples in relationships say they love their partner, but that doesn't necessarily mean that they *like* each other. Some couples have a need to stay together in unfulfilling relationships out of fear of their 'wills': "Will I ever find another to love?", "Will I ever be loved again?"

I desire a life partner with whom I can feel peace, pleasure, security, loyalty, and empathy. These are the attainable features that I look for. I don't waste my time trying to change someone and neither should you, because whatever you give, ought to be returned freely. Besides, if he changes for you and not himself, the change may not last. Love that is unconditional, unfailing, and unselfish is an important element in the concept of *self-love*.

What's your desire for your love life? If you can answer this question, then how did you get to the place where you are, with someone whom you love, but don't like?

Take relationships in steps. Don't rush love. You must get to know a person first, then develop a true liking for them and only after that can you realistically decide whether you should love him.

Freedom Comes With Taking Ownership!

When the love of another finds you, it is my prayer that their love brings you contentment. Love is healthy, enthusiastic, passionate, romantic, tender, and kind. To quote my Mother "you are perfection". You must realize, know and believe this, because there is no one that can be a more perfect 'you' than you.

Try adoring the person that is always with you when you're alone. That's you! There is a reason for you to love your self. Without this affection and admiration it is impossible for you to know your self worth. It should matter to you that someone with whom you share an intimate relationship celebrates your perfection by acknowledging your fineness. By loving yourself most of all, you will have the surety to effectively choose an intimate partner. What you see in your self, is what everyone else will see. Ultimately, it's your choice to show others how you want to be treated, by how you treat yourself. Make a promise to adore the person you are, for the rest of your life.

A peaceful mind is a mind without the fear of failure, because it's certain to try again. Don't let inadequate or destructive communications disturb that peacefulness of spirit. Find intimacy within yourself. You are the cake and anyone that joins with your spirit should be just the icing.

What is 'love' and why do we have the need to say that we feel it? Why is it, that these four letters of the alphabet cause so many emotions when put together in one small, yet powerful word? Just hearing it spoken by the right person can cause the blood to flow faster, our tear ducts to open, and our stomach to tie in knots. Sometimes it's so overwhelming that we think the cramping will never stop and the passion ignited by the word itself can feel like a sword in the side. But when spoken by someone we have no interest in, it's just a word, a sound made with the voice and four ordinary letters that have no exceptional power.

The letters themselves aren't any more powerful than others. When put together and spoken, it is the receiver who gives the word its power.

Chapter 3

Does It Really Matter?

So what? You agreed to sleep with someone that you really liked. The person said all the things that made you feel the time was right and you thought the sex was the best you've ever had. You felt it all- endless love, you saw the stars and landed smack-dab on the moon. The passion singed the very depths of your soul. Your eyes rolled back in your head and you nearly climbed the walls. The last thing you remember is strange sounds coming from your mouth that vaguely reminded you of someone speaking in tongues. And the morning after, your beloved couldn't even remember your name. *Does it really matter?*

Usually, it does. In most cases, you find yourself getting upset and feeling as if you loaned your body out and it came back used. Why do you feel so wounded? You enjoyed yourself, didn't you? Don't be confused when you have good sex and *think* that someone has touched your heart. Ask any doctor whether your heart is in your skirt or your pants and they'll undoubtedly say, "Of course not."

If you're not willing to give your heart, can it be touched during sex? Not by a physical act, it can't. Nor can it be touched by emotion, unless it was freely given. Remember, he didn't take anything from you that you weren't willing to give. Next time, say to yourself *"That was just good sex for the night, but I want a friendship for life."*

We can all understand the craving for love, but how many are willing to work on the changes needed to open ourselves to love from someone we truly want? We groom ourselves for pro- motions and goals. We get training to be ready for our dream job.

Why not prepare our selves for love? Are you ready for love if it comes your way, and if it does, are you confident you can keep it?

Knowing full well that love can be emotionally testing, why do people desire to have love? Is it because love appears to be youthful, warm, and energetic? I once asked a stranger who looked like he was in love, what love feels like. I also asked him what he applied to the relationship, to make the love last.

He said "A relationship that isn't flourishing takes a lot of effort to make it last, but I never thought a healthy and loving relationship could take just as much work to sustain. The difference between the two is the *wills*. When a relationship is good, there is energy and a will to make it last. When it's bad, the desire to will the relationship to last sometimes is lost, leaving it hopeless. Love takes nurturing, being flexible, and compromising at times. It is exhausting and frustrating, but rewarding and fulfilling. Love is being comfortable with who you share the love with."

"Well put," I say.

You can walk away from a one-night stand or a broken relationship, torn and hurt, or you can leave realizing its importance in gaining clarity and confirmation of what the sexual act meant to the both of you before you had sex. Feeling used and depressed, as though you were taken advantage of, can have a negative effect on you physically, mentally, and socially to the point where you start to distrust the love of family and friends. You close the spiritual door, putting all sorts of locks in place so the next roaming heart won't be able to open it without entering the right combination or finding all the concealed keys. This barricade may work, but it would be as well to remember a song about the challenges of relationships performed by Betty Wright- "No Pain, No Gain," she sings, "In order to get something, you've got to give something." When you close the door to your heart, it could hinder your capabilities for caring, trusting, and simply living. A shut door may keep others from getting in, but remember a door swings both ways—you could be preventing yourself from getting out.

The results of your "change" can have a "cause and effect" reaction that means you begin to attract superficial people, which may in fact be the type of person you have become. Any relationships you have at this point may go nowhere quickly and leave you yearning for the real thing, someone who *desires* to have your love and friendship for life. To your friends you start sounding like a hopeless romantic. No one wants to be around you because they are afraid of being infected with your illness. This illness is what I call a D.I.C. problem.

A person without a D.I.C. problem takes ownership of her choice, so her reaction to a one-night stand is different. She knows that a sexcapade is not love and recognized this fact long before she ever went to bed with someone.

A person who practices D.I.C. skills knows that love is healthy, enthusiastic, passionate, romantic, tender, and kind. This person would work hard not to allow destructive communication to enter into the spirit of her relationship. She has learned either from her friends or past relationships that she must first find intimacy within herself before she can communicate intimacy to someone else. In doing this, she has come to understand that she is in control of her own happiness. It's not up to her partner to make her feel complete. She would never put the blame on someone else for a failure. By taking full responsibility for her actions, she minimizes the fuzzy, gray areas

that could have easily screwed up the foundation of a relationship.

A person who takes command of her choices wakes up
much happier than someone who doesn't, because there is less
uncertainty in her life. She has honestly given thought to the
type of relationship she wants and if the other person is not
responding in an appropriate manner, she knows it is time to
move on.

I must admit, I like people with good D.I.C. skills. They
just lay their expectations, perceptions, desires, and wants out in
the open. They stand out from everyone else, and they know it.
They are in love with themselves, and if a relationship fails, they
are still open and willing to give love to others.

I called this book *Teaching the D.I.C. (Discipline of Intimacy
and Communication)* for many reasons. One, I wanted a title that
would make great dinner-table conversation. The title, *Teaching
the D.I.C.,* is intriguing enough to entice readers to pick it up, and
the content is designed to not only make them think about it, but
discuss its concepts with others. This book is informal and
meant to be accessible, which allows for more intimacy, and

D.I.C. encourages conversation and dialogue (but, let's call it communication for the purpose of this book).

Intimate conversation is important to me. Speaking one's thoughts is therapeutic. What you say and how you say it can have a lasting effect on a person. Wrongly worded advice for example, can cause someone to fight a psychological battle forever—even if the advice is constructive.

I've seen this type of conflict take place in people, many times throughout my life. As a child, I was a victim of poorly presented constructive criticism. During an assignment in the third grade, my teacher told me to go to the chalkboard and write the next sentence. As I began, she interrupted me in a loud voice, complaining that my handwriting looked like "chicken scratching." Of course, there was an immediate burst of laughter from my classmates. Whenever I was required to write as a child, I would print and still do today. Even though that incident took place decades ago, I learned that an effective exchange of dialogue is the cornerstone of our everyday life. Those who master it, go further and are usually happier. With greater social intimacy, a person is less confused about the direction of their life. One of the reasons a baby cries is because he has not learned to converse effectively.   Communication, according to Webster's Dictionary, is the instance of sharing or the exchanging of information, feelings, thoughts, or wishes. The key words in this definition are *sharing* and *exchanging*. They are action words that mean to give in return for something received.

You can ask a baby all day long if he is hungry but he will never be able to effectively share a verbal exchange with you. By the same token, if you decide to sleep with someone to whom you have not communicated your feelings, thoughts, or wishes, why would you think that the two of you are truly being intimate? Some people may say that having sex is being intimate, but I see that as no more intimate than a handshake with a perfect stranger.   Intimate means to have very close association or familiarity with someone.   True, sex and a handshake may constitute a close association, but if nothing more than a touch is exchanged then it's just like any other meaningless sexual act or careless handshake. You can walk through the great pyramids of Egypt a thousand times and never be truly familiar with them. It may take you years before you ever totally know just one pyramid.

Another reason I titled this book *Teaching the D.I.C. (Discipline of Intimacy and Communication)* is to give the reader a tool to use when, or if, you find yourself in some of the situations that I mention. Hopefully, you will then be able to take control, with good discipline, confidence, and respect. By doing so, you can make more prudent decisions about the outcomes that you would really like to see in your life.

Lying on top of another person with your clothes off, wondering what it means, because you never asked what your mate's true feelings are, is not being intimate. It's operating on an assumption and not confirmation. This is obvious because you are not utilizing good D.I.C. skills. If you become disciplined enough to allow a person to know the real you before hopping into bed with him, then you'll find that your relationship will be much more satisfying.

Many of you who feel your relationships never seem to go anywhere as a result of not being compromising, pleasing, kind, or desirable enough, may find to your surprise, that you are capable of being liked. By using good D.I.C. to get to know you, by spending time learning what gives you pleasure, by truly understanding your passion, dislikes, and expectations, you and your prospective partner will find love.

(Poem) Why Do I Wonder?

Why do **I wonder...**
if you feel
    if you care
        if you need
            if you want
Or even that you...
feel
  care
    need
      want
Why do **I think** I know...
how you feel
    that you care
        when you need
            what you want

Part I: So, You Think You Know Yourself...

Why do **I guess**...
you feel
    you care
        you need
            you want
Why do **I assume** you...
feel
  care
    need
      want
Why do **I wonder?**
    Why do **I think?**
        Why do **I guess?**
           Why do **I assume?**
      Why?
    Why?
Why don't I ask?
    I wonder why I am content with not knowing.
           Is it that to know the truth would loose the
           restraints within my mind and the woes of
           my soul?
   What is it that makes me afraid of knowing
           the truth if it could eventually set me free?
        Truth doesn't take thought, time, or delay.
   It is a constant—a continual state of being.
        One might say that truth can set me free,
          free is in the mind and in the soul.
   Truth may cause pain that lasts
        a day or may be an overnight stay.
       Not like the pain from deception
           that can cause permanent scars
             that may never pass away.

        Sooooo, again I ask...
        Why Do I Wonder?

        Author: Terry Smith

Chapter 4

Why Do We Wonder?

Sometimes our assumptions are all in the way we see things. Today, I passed by a man who appeared to be homeless. "Oh, wow!" I thought. "That old man is someone's father." Without confirmation, my thought is an assumption. All I can be certain of, is that he is someone's son.

Of course we wonder about some things that only time, life experiences, and maturity can answer. One of the most deep-seated mysteries of all time is love. What is love? Can one really experience love, without it being returned or without someone to love? My personal belief is yes, you can love without it being returned or without having someone to love. If you get satisfaction from self-love, then you understand that you have love even without the love of others. Love is a personal emotion.

We all have areas that we find uncomfortable to discuss. For example, we usually shy away from asking someone how much money he makes, or about his sexual preference and past sexual experiences. We assume that all women want to have children, or all men are breadwinners. Even after dining, if a man is present, most often the assumption is that the check goes to him.

If looking through a crystal ball could reveal everything in your future, would you look? With just a glance, you would know your true love and eliminate all of the lessons and different experiences that could help to better prepare you for Mr. Right and keep you from dating Mr. Wrong. You wouldn't have to wonder who your real friends were, because you would know. There would be no more doubt. Your entire future could be revealed *but* you would have no choice as to what the crystal ball reveals. The ball can eliminate all doubts and assumptions and reveal all your truths, love, happiness, joy, and peace as well as your pain and sorrow. Would you want to glance in the crystal ball?

Why do we wonder? One reason might be because we are afraid of being told things we don't want to hear. In the past, you may have raised certain questions to a partner and because of his unexpected response, you are afraid to ask someone else the same question.

Some people find comfort in assuming the possible answers to their questions. Another reason for not asking questions may stem from the lack of discipline, intimacy and communication skills. You may be afraid of the truth and the unknown. Wondering can be viewed as the waiting period you give yourself in hopes that the truth of what you want to know will come to light on its own. That leads to another reason why we wonder: we are waiting for the answer to fall in our laps. Nevertheless, many of us are craving the truth, without the skill to ask for it.

In certain circumstances, some people may intentionally avoid the truth. For instance, when we are ill, many of us avoid going to the doctor for fear of hearing the diagnosis. There's an old saying, "Don't ask what you don't want asked of you!" Sometimes we protect someone's heart by not telling the truth when asked certain questions. But the truth is, we may not want to know the answer to those questions ourselves. Sometimes even when *truth* is revealed, leaving no doubt, you can hear it, see it, or smell it—we simply don't believe it.

Is wondering easier? No! Assuming someone cares for us is a comfortable state of mind that we all default to until we are ready to be challenged with learning the truth. Does wondering make it easier to live without certainty? Guessing offers limitless possibilities, making wondering bearable, even acceptable. One might say that wondering gives us a moment of contentment. During the waiting period, we can look for the inner strength to ask what our mind has been questioning.

If there is no confirmation, then we are left with an assumption, and an assumption is still a guess that lacks certainty. When we say, "There is no need to ask because I already know that he'll say 'no' as usual," it does not resolve the question, but simply justifies the answer in our heart. The only problem is that our assumption may not be truth.

Some people, typically those with aggressive personalities, can be comfortable asking questions to gain clarity. Individuals with a more cautious personality however, may feel uncomfortable asking questions because they are careful not to cause conflict. All personality types may not ask questions out of concern for someone's feelings, or because the timing could be inappropriate.

There are people who go through life wondering about such things as who their biological parents are. Men have been known to accept the responsibility of a child they are not certain is theirs. Some individuals *hope* that their love for another person is returned. Again, none of them have the strength to ask for the truth.

So what can we do to improve communication? First, before asking a question, it must be clear in your own mind, what your goal is. Think of your reason(s) for asking, and then seek information in a way that is certain to accomplish your goal.

Structure the question in a way that results in dialogue. For example: "How do you feel about..." or "Can you explain...?"

The result should be an answer that eliminates doubt.

The Pinstriped Party Dress

When you give a gift to someone, do you want to know or not if you captured the essence of the person with the gift you gave? Does it bother you when you give someone a present and never see him use it, especially when he initially said how much he liked it?

If someone cares enough to give you a gift, something that he took considerable time and effort to pick out especially for you, would you tell him if it really wasn't your taste, or it didn't fit? Or would you stick it in the attic with other gifts you didn't like to then give it to someone else? If you said you would not tell the person, why not? If you were the gift giver, would you want to know if the receiver did not care for the gift or if it didn't fit?

Why does a wife tell her husband that she loves the pinstriped party dress with polka-dot ruffle trim when she knows that she will never wear it? Not telling her husband the truth, will actually encourage him to continue buying the wrong gifts, and she will have unused presents piling up in the back of her closet.

Does she not tell her husband for fear that it may lead him to be honest with her the next time she doesn't make a perfect gift selection for him? Or is it by being untruthful, she protects her husband's heart? Some people always respond to receiving gifts with appreciation, even if it's superficial, because they expect others to respond in the same way (grateful).

Sometimes kind acts can end up being hurtful. If the giver never sees their gifts, you may appear dishonest or ungrateful. The gift giver could stop caring. He may no longer make an effort to give anything, even his love.

A Case in Point

It's your wedding day, and you and your partner are standing at the altar before family and friends. Some wedding guests have traveled a long way to witness the two of you uniting as one. The ceremony has all the traditional trimmings. The only thing needed to seal the union, is to say, "I do". As you turn to give the nod, a question comes to mind. It is one that you have often thought about, but never asked. Until then, you have been content with just wondering; however, you now find it difficult to concentrate on this most important event with the issue unresolved.

You struggle with the thought that asking this question may result in a range of answers, some of which you aren't prepared to handle. You feel this question could change the mood of the event, your mind, or your partner's mind. On the one hand, the right answer would heighten the moment; on the other, you might hear an answer that delays your decision to go through with the ceremony now or forever.

To Ask or Not

The feelings are mutual... the two of you feel the desire to be sexually intimate. The mood is set, the candles are lit, the music is low, the two of you are slowly moving toward the bedroom and the bed is adorned with velvety red rose petals.

After passionately undressing each other, the mood intensifies, and a question that you've wondered about comes to mind. What will this relationship mean to your partner after this moment? You think, "If I ask, it could change the mood; but if I don't ask, I may have regrets about what is about to happen." With everything set so right, do you follow through with the mood or do you ask the question? Is this an appropriate moment, or is this bad timing that could cost you the relationship?

I've talked about this scenario to many people who have been in similar situations. Some struggled with the decision of whether to ask the question. You're really thinking, "What does this mean to him?" You're guessing this intimate sexual moment matters. You're assuming that the person cares.

Is there ever a place or time where it is inappropriate to ask an important question? The consequence of asking very intimate things is not evident until after the response. If you don't ask the question, will you be filled with deep regret? If you do ask the question, will it change the mood? Would you prefer to live your life asking questions or always doubting? You've probably heard married people say that if they had only asked about their spouse's expectations, they wouldn't have married them. Some individuals agreed they didn't ask a question while standing next to their life mate at the altar, because they felt it wasn't the appropriate time. I asked them, if preparing to make what is expected to be a lifetime commitment is not an appropriate moment, what is?

One unhappily wedded man's response was "Today if I had known what I found out later, even at the moment before I said 'I do', I would have stopped the ceremony and cleared up any assumptions."

Why would we ever feel that there is an inappropriate time to ask questions that may change our lives? There are circumstances or situations, that can make the moment seem like the question is inappropriate. But asking the question may make things less stressful and more enjoyable. More importantly, it could provide the clarity needed to make the right decision. Sometimes unplanned moments can be the best time to ask important questions, because they are least expected and the response is spontaneously genuine. Even a con artist can be thrown off, when asked something at an unexpected moment.

Often, the way you structure a question results in an offhand response. That kind of answer may not provide the confirmation you're looking for. My reasons for not asking yes-or-no questions is if you ask a question like 'do you love me', you will get a short positive or negative answer. If you ask in a way that requires explanation or reason—like "why do you love me?" —you may feel more confident with the response, and can then make the right decision.

I have always been a strong communicator, especially in intimate settings. The first time I asked a man "What does our having sex mean to you?" I was shocked by what happened. The mood immediately changed. My partner got up out of the bed and started getting dressed. While he was pulling the shirt over his head, I asked, "What are you doing?" He muttered, "I'm going home." In disbelief, but just so I was clear, I repeated what I thought I'd heard him say, " You're going home? Why? What's wrong?" His response was even more shocking than the sudden mood change. "'What does this mean to me' is a question I don't know how to answer."

"Why? Just answer it!" I said.

He replied, "If I say it's just sex, that seems shallow and I don't think of myself as shallow. If I say it's more than sex, then what commitment am I making to the relationship?" He also stated that the question changed the mood and he felt that it was an inappropriate time to ask it. He gave me a gentle kiss on the lips and left. I stood staring at the closed door thinking, *I guess he had a headache....*

I was having lunch with a male co-worker the next day and told him what happened. After he stopped laughing, he volunteered his opinion. He said that my partner was anticipating the feeling of ecstasy. When I asked what the sex meant to him, the man had a hard time thinking with his brain, instead of his hormones. Hearing that question at an unplanned moment put pressure on him. He may have been wondering, "Is this a trick?" or "How do I answer in a way that ensures we'll still have sex?" My co-worker ended his opinion with this statement: "It seems obvious that your mate cares for you, because he left the situation in order to take some quality time and consider his answer."

When we look at a few synonyms for the word 'communication' you find 'interface, interchange, and social intercourse'. On that day my partner and I didn't even have social intercourse. Because of the way I had asked the question, it required D.I.C. skills on both of our parts. My goal in asking was to gain clarity by way of conversation and communication. He answered with the best response he could honestly give at that time. Not knowing what his feelings were concerning our sexual intimacy, he took the time that he needed, alone, to figure it out.

When he left, I took time to reflect on what part I played in the anticipated exchange of passion that didn't happen. I wondered if my reason for asking him to clarify his feelings about us making love (at that moment), was because I simply wanted the assurance his answer would give, to make me feel as though our intimacy was worthy of this level of pleasure.

I spent time in thought. I thought about all the possible reasons for what was intended, not to happen. Did I want making love to define our relationship as exclusive? Or was my motive in not wanting it to be more than a shared closeness? I wondered how long I had wanted to know what his feelings were concerning our expected night of pleasure. There was no denying the passion. It was so hot that it had reached its boiling point and I wanted to explode. But, even with the intensity of the moment, I was uncertain what our making love meant to our relationship. He could have felt that expressing our feelings by making love, solidified his commitment to the relationship. All these doubts clearly indicate indecisiveness.

I reflected on my Mother's words of wisdom about taking responsibility for my decisions because I have to live with them. I was certain: I wasn't going to have any unanswered questions even if the timing was inappropriate. I asked the question so I could know exactly what he was feeling. Once he walked out the door, I knew there was a chance that he may never return. Even with possibility of that happening, I had no regrets for asking the question or for the timing. I never regret asking a question that eliminates guessing, gathers facts or leads to an enlightening conversation. The answer could mean I am comfortable in making a decision that I will be content with.

The outcome to our story is my partner returned with an answer that made him feel good about himself and us as a couple. I was happy with the response and the passion began again.

Chapter 5

Finding Oneself—The Journey

My Mother instilled in me the importance of loving myself, finding my power within and that I should never, ever give up my will to someone else. I absorbed those words and began a journey to discover what kind of person I wanted to be, and how I wanted others to see me. After some time, I realized I wanted to be thought of as kind, willing to be inconvenienced for others, confident, fearless and unstoppable. In the attempt to find my self I had my first sexual experience.

It was disappointing, to say the least. No communication, just hands, feet and legs everywhere. Once the sexual mischief was over I came away wondering what all the hype was about. Someone twice your weight, lying on top of you, pressing on your tender underdeveloped breasts and trying to be excited about his little slow moving turtle head. He was my high school sweetheart, what girls of the millennium would consider the bomb, the man, the "end all – be all" of manliness. If you were with him, you were the envied girl on campus, but to me the ambiance was different.

I dated my high school boyfriend from the ninth grade to the twelfth. He was romantic – really. He gave me flowers and candy all the time, wrote me poems and never forgot a holiday. I got my first diamond ring from him, a beautiful diamond chip centered in a 10-karat gold band. Oh, and don't think he was a schmuck...no, not my guy! He even got a job at McDonalds so he could buy a car to sport me around in. I knew the car wasn't perfect—to be perfect, the car would have had the capability of going in reverse, which it didn't. Whenever the car was stuck, he simply explained that the car not being able to go into reverse wasn't a problem because most of the time our goal was to drive forward. Sometimes he'd get out and push the car, but overall the inconvenience really didn't bother me. He worked hard to give me the best. I assumed he really loved me, you know... in the naïve, carefree way high school kids love each other. In high school there are no cares about the important stuff, like your future, world peace or whose turn it is to take out the trash. Like most girls my age, I was maturing faster than my male counterparts and losing interest in a high school boy. I refocused my sights on college boys... future doctors, and lawyers or simply, someone who had a credit card. You must forgive me. I was just eighteen. By the end of my senior year the relationship ended, because there was no Discipline of Intimacy and Communication between us. So, after graduation I moved on, carrying only the fond memories of my first boyfriend.

Shortly after graduation, Mother moved us to Virginia. Now we were three; my brother had already matriculated at a college in Virginia and Daddy was living there with his new wife. I'm sure the distance had caused a strain on my parent's parenting relationship. I'm sure the communications between them were worse than it appeared at the time. My Mother confessed that she and my father discussed having children and the responsibility that brought, but they never talked about their expectations of the marriage. However, I will give my parents credit, because they never entangled us in the drama of their divorce. For the most part they hid everything from us. They never actually told us why they got a divorce. For a long time, I blamed my Mother, thinking that she must have done something really bad to make my daddy leave me. As an adult, I've come to see my father in a different light. He isn't the perfect man I'd always believed him to be. (He may have been a good father... but he was not a good husband.) Now on his third marriage, I have begun to see a pattern. Every time he goes through a divorce he remarries within three months of the last divorce. The other woman... I know. My Mother probably knew more about why my daddy left, than she ever told us.

When we moved to Virginia my parents had "words", but they were civil. The truth is, when it came down to the children, (they still refer to us as the children) my parents worked together. There are many people from two-parent homes, who can't say that their parents supported each other when it came to issues involving their children.

Shortly after arriving in Virginia, I got a job with a local company that paid extremely well. Securing a position with this company would have been difficult on my own, but my daddy had inside connections. He played a big role in securing that job for me. I remember my Mother saying, "Know your power". In this case, since my father had influence and because I was his child, I also had the power. I had only worked a month when I met the man that I would later marry. He was my first love.

It was the middle of the workweek, a glorious, sunny summer morning. I had one of my--this day is going to be a great day, feelings. Every hair was in place. I'd just bought this great new outfit that curved perfectly with my body. A classic Ann

Taylor business blouse, fitted skirt and Aigner pumps. As I stepped out of my baby blue convertible Volkswagen Rabbit I placed my matching suit jacket on my left arm. I was just about to close the car door, when I saw him for the first time! Out of the corner of my eye quite some distance away, I could see him coming toward me. I took a split second to weigh the pros and cons--Giorgio Armani or Bill Blass. Should I pretend to look for something in my car--the back seat and then the front--to buy time for him to catch up? Yes! I can't see the ring finger from here, I thought, looking through my back window while stooping inside my car. He could be single or married, or *married*, but only when he's with his wife. He could have a dazzling or cunning smile or he could be a man with several hateful ex-wives that he's paying an enormous amount of alimony to support. The split second was turning into more time than I had to waste. I shut the door and started walking toward the building and within two steps he was next to me, extending his hand and introducing himself. I didn't hear him at first. I was thinking he must have been walking extremely fast because he was almost a football field away a minute ago. Then I took a second to look at him and collect my thoughts. "Most definitely all the pros... pros and Bill Blass." I said "Hello," and introduced myself to him. I can't emphasize enough, how beautifully sunny the morning was. To date, I have never seen a more perfect day. We walked the rest of the way side by side and in some ways we have been together ever since. Later, I found out that he had sprinted the last 20 yards to catch me because he was attracted by my legs even at a distance. He also told me he had said to himself "I've got to know those legs" and since the rest of me was attached to them, he got to know all of me.

Our relationship wasn't love at first site. I thought of him more like my mentor and I was the student. He was seven years my senior, and I can vividly remember our first date. There was a gospel concert that night at my church. I asked if he would like to join our family for dinner before the concert and if he would escort me to the church afterwards. He was very impressed to hear that I had a spiritual background and was pleased to receive any invitation that included food. He was slim, 6'2" well-groomed man who loved home cooked meals, and accepted readily. (Being from the South, Sundays with the family is a given and you're sure to enjoy a big dinner spread.)

I fried chicken, cooked a roast of beef, and browned onions, mixed with a little flour & water to make the perfect gravy. Uncle Ben's rice, three cheese macaroni and cheese with toasted bread crumbs sprinkled over the top, green beans, Jiffy cornbread with a touch of sugar added, homemade rolls and to drink - Cherry Kool-Aid. My family wasn't big on desserts, so I bought a sweet potato pie from the corner bakery and placed the pie in the oven to burn the top and give the crust a home made look. After dinner we went to the concert. The visiting choir was dynamic, the choir director and lead vocalist, icing on the cake. I got a good feeling when I saw him clapping and really enjoying the recital. My heart warms to see a man interested in a church service. This made knowing him better seem *very* worthwhile.

I've always felt that connecting spiritually is important, but it is only one thing that is important to me. There are many more on a long list of friendship requirements like... kindness, loyalty, and empathy. As well as someone that is strong enough to articulate his wants, goals, and who feels confident in his/herself that these wants and goals "will" be attained.

The ride back home was pleasant. We talked about the service, and how the choir director seemed as if he was going to fall off the tiny stage every time he was filled with the spirit and jumped up and down. The night sky was clear and every star was visible. He pointed out constellations and told me how only some are visible in the summer and how others were visible in the winter. As I was looking at the stars, I could still see him checking me out. His interest in me made me feel good and I thought, almost in a daze, "another perfect day." But all good things must come to an end, or at least a pause. While we walked to the door, I could tell by his playful gestures that he wanted to kiss me, but was nervous. Him having jitters was understandable, because we had just left a Sanctified Church and any smart man would not want to screw up his church-going image by trying to get his groove on so soon after feeling the spirit. I know I was feeling the spirit of passion and I hoped he could hear that same spirit saying, "Please kiss me." He gave me a hug and said "Thanks for inviting me. I had a great time and thank your Mother for dinner. It was delicious." I said "You're welcome, but I cooked dinner." "Yea right," he said. "I really did do all the cooking." Still not convinced he said "I guess I'll be going." While he was turning to walk away, I don't know what came over me; maybe my assertiveness was some sort of confused hormone. I grabbed his tightly woven silk tie, pulling it towards me and kissed him. A satisfied smile spread across his face. The kiss was great, the date wonderful, and the night memorable.

Chapter 6

Teaching the D.I.C.
Student and the Mentor

My first love was without a doubt my mentor, and I his student. He had great D.I.C. skills. When we talked about life experiences he realized how naïve I was. He never let on, but I could tell. I felt comfortable in asking him my most personal questions, the kind that would cause your parents, best friend and even the sex education teacher to blush (even with a dark complexion). He would look at me and smile, then try his best to answer the question. Sometimes he would ask, "You're kidding, right?" He was very protective of me and that was always comforting.

When a good friend tells you of their interest in someone new, your response to the information can easily sound like an interrogation—how long have you known them? What do they do? What qualities do they have that make them the one...etc. But when you are the one in a new relationship, you should interview yourself, because you're the only one who can supply the answers to the same questions you'd ask someone else.

I would ask myself these questions: Would I choose this person as a friend? Do I like this person and everything he stands for? Is this association based on fairness? Do I get back the effort, interest and concern that I put into the relationship? Can I keep my power while he maintains his? Will there be a power struggle? Is he considerate and fair to mankind? These are very good questions to ask yourself in a new relationship. If a person is only kind to you and not others, they could turn on you and not be kind at any time. Ask yourself: is this person genuinely kind? Are our sexual desires the same? Is honesty and loyalty something that they require in a friend? If you are in a relationship with a person that you think is honest and loyal and their friends aren't---something's wrong. Remember, "by their friends, shall you know them," birds of a feather...you know, whatever.

While asking myself these questions as well as thousands of others, I realized that I really liked this person. Sure, I admired and trusted him, but more important to me was "like". All of them are a part of Intimate Communication, but "like" is my foundation.

So many books and studies say that love is the core of a fulfilling relationship. Why is this so? I disagree. Sometimes when we love we are in a state of bliss and can be blinded by the obvious flaws of another, and the lack of "like" or compatibility. If we are in the "like" stage, (a common foundation) we may be able to see the actions of the other person more clearly.

I was conducting a "Teaching the D.I.C." seminar for single and engaged couples. The topic was "What are the foundations of a lasting relationship?" Compatibility, love and commitment are just three elements that are important in the marriage relationship. Would you agree? I asked a question,

Part I: So, You Think You Know Yourself...

"How would you rank compatibility, love and commitment in order of importance to a marriage?" Most answered love first, compatibility second, and commitment last.   Others chose, compatibility, love then commitment. There's no right or wrong answer to the question. Your response depends on your personal feelings.   Here is how I perceive the importance of the same elements.

I think of relationships as starting with two people that have something in common, which creates a bond, leading to compatibility.

Compatibility of some sort (hobbies, work, family and friends... etc.) can be the glue that cements the foundation of a relationship together. So for me, being compatible first is most important.

Hopefully before the marriage ceremony, there is a commitment to love, and the process of the ceremony is just a reconfirmation of the commitment to love, honor and cherish. So, how can we love before we like?

How can delicate plant stems stand in the windy springtime weather without the process of a nurtured beginning, the stability of strong roots to assist in the blossoming of beautiful flowers? A relationship blooms in the same way as a flower. Therefore, you may agree that it is unlikely for love to be the core (the root, the origin) of a budding relationship, but rather the wonderful blossom which results from it.

Every foundation must be laid in an orderly manner, taking into account that its goal is to support what is above it, forever. Have you ever seen a plant leaning out of the soil, its roots exposed, because it anchored itself in an environment that can't support its ongoing need for water and sustenance? Without the proper water and nutrition the root along with the flower is sure to wither and die. There are so many layers that build from the core of a relationship. If love is the core, do we start with love first and then build? First there should be compatibility and like then the commitment to love.

In my relationship with my mentor, we didn't become lovers at first, even though there was a very strong attraction. There was so much more that we had in common, other then sex. He was from the South and I am from the South. He has a spiritual foundation and so do I. We both have a strong love of family. He has the utmost respect for all of mankind that I also share.

Even though he was a country guy, he had a big city style and plenty of charisma. He could put on a suit and ladies would think they were looking at a model straight out of GQ Magazine. His stunning, all thirty-two teeth smile, was topped off with light brown windows to the soul. His "girlfriend characteristics"— empathic, gentle, flexible were quite impressive, too. He had loyalty, ethics, honesty, and he would tell me when I was wrong, but never in front of someone. When he said something, you could rest assured that he meant it. He owned a three-bedroom split-level brick house, with a sports car and a credit card. He worked on the third floor of our company in the accounting department and yes, he was a CPA with two additional degrees.

I was working half days while still in school. We didn't let on to co-workers that we were growing closer than just friends. You know how office romances can be- so similar to a Hollywood affair. If anyone knows about the affair, other than the two involved, then the details pertaining to the relationship become everyone's business. The irony of us as individuals, was how the people in our departments would try to get us together. They thought we would make a perfect match, but we tried to act uninterested. We spent many evenings laughing about how we had skipped the "middle man" and gone directly to each other on our own.

With him I felt like one of the fellows...you know a beer buddy or a comrade, except when he kissed me. I never felt like one of the fellows then. Our feelings for one another were warmer than you could ever imagine. He always took his time as if he wanted to absorb the turbulence of my every breath. We did everything together, not because we were dating, but because when I wanted to do things with a friend, he was the friend I wanted. I always felt welcome around him, and he was excited to be around me. He loved life and rarely ever complained. He was a realist. I learned a great deal about having values just from being around him. I observed his kindness to others that he interacted with, on levels outside of our romance.

The man I loved had a child, and even though I wasn't in the picture when he and the mother of his child separated as a couple, they always worked together (because of D.I.C.) to do what was best for their daughter. Even though my parents are divorced, the lines of communication are always open for the sake of us, "their children". Experiencing my parents' relationship and the relationship between the man I loved and his ex-girlfriend, enabled me to witness the fact that just because love has changed, doesn't mean that the D.I.C. can't remain. We stayed friends for two years, dated for two and got married in the fifth year of our relationship. In the five years of our courtship, I found my best friend, my true love. He didn't change me, he enhanced me.

Chapter 7

Our Fixation with Love

Sometimes when a person is in a damaging relationship, they can't grasp that it is destructive until they see themselves as they appear to others. In the words of someone else, you can often find your own reflection. How can it be love when it hurts? It's clear from that one comment/self-question, that there's no practice of D.I.C., because you haven't communicated your hurt to your partner.

Why are so many of us unhappy in relationships? How and why do we dislike, yet love our mate? Why have we come to the realization that we have nothing in common only after we are married with children? One reason may be, because we're resigned to having less in common with a mate than a friend. What do you have in common with your friends and special partner other than the obvious? Look for answers only you would know, by asking questions and observing.

Someone once told me the hardest thing to keep in life is a friend - so true. Think about one person (besides your significant other) that you would call a best friend...not just a friend, but *best*. What is it—the thing, the reason that makes you think of them as a best friend other than the obvious? Most of the time with women, our best friend is of the same sex. Because we share similar experiences, common desires, and are considered to be natural nurturers. So what's obvious with a mate may not be obvious with a best friend. Being a best friend requires a great deal of commitment, loyalty, understanding, fairness, support and yes...an open door policy. We require more D.I.C. from a friend than the person we would later call a mate.

Think about this- when some people choose a mate, they accept much less compatibility than they would in a best friend. If you look at the elements that allow us to call someone a best friend, often times the root that makes friendships last, is that we truly like the person.

I heard a parent say, "I love my child, but I can't say I like him". I am sure this parent isn't alone in those feelings. Frustrations and disappointments are natural feelings that a parent can have when raising their family. (At times you can feel as though you dislike or are unhappy with the child.) The same holds true for the feelings of disappointment we experience, when it comes to relationships between couples. People have said, "I love my mate, but I can't say I like him."

Of course, it's expected that parents love their children, and life would be perfect if they liked them too. But perfection is fantasy in some families. Thankfully, most parents don't divorce their children. Sometimes perfection comes through the journey to maturity, when their children become adults or when they see the grandchildren that their children have blessed them with. It may not be until the journey is almost completed, that some parents realize the few dissatisfying moments of childhood, were all worth the joy of knowing their children as adults. And at last, they begin to genuinely love "liking" their children.

In seeking a mate, we often don't know much about the person before entering into a relationship. We usually know more about someone before calling them a best friend. This is mainly because "friendship takes a long time to build", and what we learn during that time, creates a bond that can last forever. People who enter into a relationship without that "prep" time, find out later when the love is tested, that they really don't like their mate. When the lust is gone they wonder what they saw in the person to start with. That's because a foundation of friendship was never built. The truth is, we know more about a person before calling them a best friend. But the question is "Why?" The answer? Because "friendship is a discipline."

To intimately understand this statement, let's explore the original definition of the root words. Friend – a person whom one knows, Discipline – Training expected to produce a specific type or pattern of behavior, training that produces moral or mental improvement, a controlled behavior resulting from training. Now, lets look at the suffix of "Friendship." "Ship" in its original Anglo-Saxon root was spelled "scip" and scip was related to the Greek word "naus" which is derived from the Latin word "nave." A nave is a part of a Gothic church, which looks a bit like a replica of the "Santa Maria" one of the ships that Columbus sailed across the ocean. Nave is where we get the words navy, nautical, and nausea. So how does it relate to friendship? Well, the nave was a confining compartment and all that were in it, were said to have been in a "scip" or a "ship" as we say it today. Thus, we get the words, Courtship, relationship, Lordship but more specifically friendship. Basically, the "ship" suffix means two or more people confined together by the boundaries of such things as love, family relations, or that of being friends.

Part I: So, You Think You Know Yourself...

Discipline in a friendship, means training yourself to develop the relationship with that person, by aggressively seeking out what makes them tick. This may seem an overly pro-active approach to what is supposed to be a bond of trust, sharing and support, but if we all took the time to learn the intimate details of a person, we would all be much happier, more confident and have great D.I.C. with the people in our friendships.

Chapter 8

Lust at First Sight

How long do we plan to live together unmarried, or is marriage the goal? Do we start out with a new place, or one of the present places and if so, do both names go on the lease? Are expenses a joint responsibility or separate? What about chores, and overnight guests? Should you get your own phone number and I get mine? If the two of us should separate, how will we divide communal possessions, debts, and savings? Let's discuss our expectations of living together.

He asked you to move in with him. Now, cohabitating before marriage isn't necessarily a bad thing. Lots of couples live together before marriage. But, with constant physical proximity, understanding of the other person's expectations is important; otherwise the arrangement can be bad D.I.C. and a relationship-ending experience.

One of my girlfriends had a magnetic attraction to a man that she met at a mid-summer wedding reception. This was unusual for her, because her ideal men were usually pinned and laid flat against a wall, 8x10 to 16x20 in size. She wanted the guy who was a poster for Mr. Right. Her preference for men was like playing the lottery. She only wanted the ones she had a one and a million chance of ever meeting in the third dimension. But, then she got lucky. This man was 6-foot and satisfying to the eye. He was definitely "eye candy", with a henna skin tone, somewhat of a George Hamilton-type, though thirty-five years younger. He was done up in a linen and silk blend suit with a white silk crewneck shirt to match. His shoes were an open-toe, wide strap, light tan leather sandal and a belt to match the unmistakable Versace outfit. She, being a girl of fashion, was wearing a provocative Dolce & Gabbana dress with shoes that matched.

The immediate attraction to this man was extremely exciting. They met at the bar while she was asking for a drink. He was standing beside her with his back leaning against the bar. You know what they say, " a bar is the wrong place to meet the right one". I say sometimes a liberal setting is also a good place, where people outside of their normal environment, are free to act or re-act as they wish, instead of how others expect.

The bartender placed her drink on the bar. She had glanced away from it for just a second, before she noticed that her drink was missing. Maybe not missing, but moving. Her glass was moving toward a pair of beautifully exquisite lips that weren't hers. Before the rim reached those lips, their owner realized that he was holding the wrong glass. He turned around and the way she described that moment to me was, "as if time stopped." They stood there staring at each other as if they knew what the other was feeling. It is said that a picture is like a thousand words, but a stare combined with a feeling can fill a book. He leaned over to her and whispered in her ear, "Would you be interested in having a heart thumping, blood boiling, sweat dripping, affair that will last an eternity?" Well that's one way to kick-start a conversation. She told me "His breath smelled so appetizing that I wanted to eat him inside out."

They couldn't take their eyes off each other, as they continued conversing. Their locked gazes stripped their souls as bare as their bodies would have been without clothes. They had no shame because they were in the privacy of their own dimension. That night they left the reception together and stayed up talking until sunrise the next morning. "He is the one," she told me the next day.

The next week was spent together. They couldn't keep their hands (not to mention other parts) off one another. They were glued at the hip, phone, and web site. Every night, it was dinner at some fancy restaurant and breakfast in bed at one of their houses. By the second week, they had announced they were in love and planning a life together. Then things began to change, a month or more into the relationship.

My friend's new man was unhappy with his job and wanted to quit, so he could take a stab at being an entrepreneur. So, having someone pay half the expenses would be a great help for him. She has always saved and planned for her future and admired others that did the same. He on the other hand lived for the moment. She said, "moving in with someone that I hardly know and helping them with their expenses isn't in my plans for the future".

The way that he lived, with no worry about tomorrow, impressed her, in the beginning. Being with someone that goes, moves, and spends at a moment's notice, can feel like a dream. But if you sleep too long, the dream can be a living nightmare.

She said "we don't have that much in common". I asked if they discussed any of the important things, when they spent that magical first night together. "We really just talked about how powerful the attraction between us was, when we saw each other. That type of attraction has never happened with anyone else before" she said. I thought 'What a cliché, definitely no D.I.C.' "I don't even feel the same passion when we're intimate, as I did at the beginning of the relationship. I'm a smart woman. I know that you can't judge a book by its cover. Before I slept with him, I should have read the pages. He is an open book. He spends like there is no tomorrow, and I save so I can have a tomorrow", she said.

Part I: So, You Think You Know Yourself...

    Love at first site... They separated! Today my girlfriend is married to a man that she calls her "soul mate". They were married three years after their first date and those dating years were spent communicating by asking question, talking about likes and dislikes, compromising some things and making their commitment, change the others. When I watch them interact with one another, it is obvious by the way that they embrace each other's opinions, that they are truly intimate.

Chapter 9

Don't Feel Obligated

"Everyone knows what real love feels like". That's a blanket, but not an accurate statement. Sadly, there are some people that have never experienced real, good, guiltless, painless or healthy love. If you are certain of when love is love and the feelings seem right to you, great! You're the type of person who won't let someone force you into saying it's love, when you know that what you are experiencing feels nothing like it. If you are someone that has felt what you think is love, and this emotion hurts or you're not sure of how love should feel, then talk with a professional- a counselor, a church pastor, or a psychologist. Someone who is trained in the relationship area, can help in your search to find a healthy love, so that you can embrace it, when it comes your way. Trust me- love will come your way, because life is about time for all things to happen, and the better your D.I.C. gets, the less time some things will take. D.I.C. is directly related to your behavior and personality. Remember, you can choose your behavior.

Make a list from 1-10 of the things that you admire and respect about your mate or the top qualities you are looking for in a mate. Separately list the things you don't like, and will not compromise on. "One" should be the most important quality your soul mate must have. Also make a note of what on the list you *are* willing to compromise on.

Look at the type of people you've been dating. See if they at least meet the top 5 requirements on the list. They likely won't, because when it comes to your needs and wants in a romantic relationship, you have been compromising. An addict won't change unless he or she is ready.

If there are things that would make you like the person more, choose a relaxed, or casual time to tell them how much you admire and respect them. Let them feel that you are on their side and not their adversary. With feeling and expression, tell them how much more you would like them if they could change this or stop doing or saying that. Smile and say that your goal is to have a solid, foundation with your best friend. This is something that often works with children, too. Then allow some time to see if there are any changes and if they are lasting.

It doesn't matter if someone tells you they love you before you are ready to return the sentiment. You should never feel obligated to say, "I love you". Rarely, do two people arrive at the same feeling, at the same time.

I love you. Do you love me too? Feel no obligation to tell someone "I love you" when you don't. Just because it is said to you, doesn't mean you are obligated to say it back. This is one of those circumstances where the cliché "its better to give then to receive" doesn't apply.

Four years ago, I made a promise to my Higher Being that if I were blessed with an inner voice that allowed me to sense what feels right or wrong, that I would listen. Today I know that if a new relationship doesn't feel right, look right, and sound right, then it probably isn't right. Don't allow anyone to pressure you into saying you love him or her, when you don't. Let them know that you need time to feel the love. You may eventually find that he is not "the one", but if he gives you time to express your feelings without pressure, it shows that he is secure and wants only what feels right for both of you. Consideration of your feelings, shows respect for you and indicates that your feelings matter to him. Take notice. Honoring your wishes also says that they respect themselves, by giving you a breathing space. Life is about choices. You have the choice to love someone or not. If you are ever feeling forced, it's not love, and the relationship may prove to be unhealthy. So stop! Let your mind, heart and soul be in harmony before any regrets cause you harm, guilt, pain, or shame.

Chapter 10

You Can Choose Your Behavior

People make conscious decisions in situations where they have control. What they are willing to do, and not do. When you ask a person for something that is in their power to make happen, they have already decided whether or not they are going to do what you've ask. They are in control of their behavior. Now you must determine how you will react, if you don't receive what you are seeking.

Freedom comes with taking ownership of your choices. If it means nothing, then let it go. You can choose to act like the hurt is not there when it is, or believe the disappointment doesn't matter when it does, or you can tell yourself *it's no big deal,* when your feelings of discontent show differently. Consider what you are going to do in this type of situation. You have to come to a decision.

I am nutty about celebrations, especially when it involves the exchanging of gifts. I can always find a cause to celebrate. When I am in a relationship, I make this very clear. I always try to find someone compatible and/or at least conscious of how important this is to me.

I dated one particular guy for a short time. He went out of his way *not* to give me what I asked for, whenever it was time to exchange gifts. It wasn't that he couldn't afford the things that I asked for, because the gifts that he chose to give me were far more expensive. The problem was, I asked for what I wanted, and his belief was that telling people what to give for a gift was inappropriate. He made his position very clear: I should allow people to give me what *they* choose. And, I should be satisfied that they thought enough of me to make that gift.

Okay. But that's not me. I believe that if you don't like making returns, let me help you eliminate the second trip. There are many relationships that would be less bumpy if the two people involved, would simply communicate and talk about what they wanted, before they bought each other things. I would get so upset with this guy. Believe me, that was our biggest problem. No, not that he wouldn't get me the gifts that I wanted- my feelings of frustration were much bigger than that. Most problems in relationships *are* larger than the obvious. He kept telling me that it was silly for me to be upset, and that I was way too serious about what gift I got from him. He was right in some ways. So I agreed, it was silly for me to get upset over his conscious decision not to give me what I wanted, and I needed to get serious and understand what message he was sending me. He was going to do things his way, no matter how I felt. Having good communication is not always enough. This guy made his position clear about how he felt and I made things clear about how I felt. Both of us were unwilling to change our stance.

Every time I said something that he felt was of no concern, he dismissed it. Even when he was not only aware, but certain of how I felt. If he didn't agree, that subject or issue would be disregarded. I told him "Some months before you met me, I began what I believe to be a cleansing of elements I don't want in a relationship and embracing the ones that I was certain I did want. I realized how crucial it was to feel that we could communicate freely, as well as have respect for each other's opinions. This realization came through prayer, faith and wanting to open my heart to someone who wants the same."

I simply said, "Honey, what you're doing hurts, mainly because the hurt is unnecessary. You can choose your behavior, but you can't regulate my emotions." I decided to take ownership and deal with what he was *not* doing. I looked at the bigger picture... together, we had bad D.I.C. And if I stayed in the relationship, I was saying yes to being disappointed every time he was not in agreement with my needs or wants. So I left him. The intimacy never materialized.

Let what you say, agree with the conscious decision you have made in your mind. Take ownership of your decisions.

I'm Listening To What You're Doing

There was another man that I dated for a few years. From time to time I would say "no" to sex. But, with the right persuasion... nibbling on the ear, passionate kisses, holding me close, whispering over and over "I want you, I need you"... gradually my nos... became yessss! Oh, come on, you weren't there! Even Mother Teresa would have digressed.

One night I was very tired. I knew by 6 p.m. that NO was going to be NO that night. You know- long day at work, traffic jams on the way home, red lights that seemed to stay red for hours. I was exhausted. I didn't even want to think and no amount of persuasion would change my mind. He called soon after I arrived home. He was on his cell phone, en route to my place, wherc we usually spent the evenings together. When we went to bed, I told him nothing was going to happen because I wanted to get some sleep. He didn't hear that. He heard "she needs the right persuasion." We went to bed at 1 a.m. and when the alarm went off at 6 a.m. I was furious. I had spent the entire night talking in my sleep- stop, no, not tonight, I'm sleepy, go to sleep, move over, stop, no...not tonight... go to sleep... I was extremely angry the next day, as well as sleepy. I didn't talk to him for two days. When I did, I said, "I told you before we went to bed, that nothing was going to happen. But you kept trying the entire night. You kept me up and I didn't get any sleep. Why didn't you listen to me?" He said "you've told me nothing was going to happen before and changed your mind, so how was I to know you meant it this time?" Touché, I replied!

Since then, I have never had a man pull that nonsense again. My NOs mean no and my YES means yes. No exceptions to the rule...

It's Not What You Say But, What You Do After You Say It

This is a good example of how the lack of D.I.C. can undermine a stable relationship... she says one thing but means another. He hears what she does, and ignores what she says.

I can't hear you because what you're doing speaks so loudly.

If you are in a relationship solely because of the benefits like money or status, and you do not have good communication, let it go and stop wasting your time.

I have girlfriends who will leave that particular door open just in case that's all that is on offer at the moment. One of my friends is a swimsuit cover model: 26 years old, 5'9" beautiful, olive-skinned, green eyes, 110 lbs. She dates, or sees... well, in her case lets just call them "sponsors".

One gentleman is twice her age, 5'7", 260 lbs, receding hairline, well manicured and has love handles that are part of the package for many men past middle age. He's someone older women would like to have by their side, and they react badly when he's seen with a woman so much younger...than them.

This guy was head over heels in love with my friend, however she didn't feel the same way about him. She made her feelings very clear to all of her other friends, me included, that she didn't want anything other than a platonic friendship. Looking on from the outside, I knew she was skating around the truth about how she felt, when she talked to him. So all the frustration that she was encountering, arose solely because what she would say and do, would contraD.I.C.t each other.

He lived on the west coast and she lived on the east coast. One day, she told him she wasn't coming out to visit. He got very upset and said "I'm not getting anything from this relationship and you don't care about me". She said, "I do care about you." He stopped ranting and raving just because he heard a morsel of what he wanted to hear, a window of hope, a small drop of affection. "You care?" he asked. "Yes I care," she said, telling him what he wanted to hear, just to placate him. "And I can come to see you later, some time next week, OK?" "OK." He said.

The next day he called with his travel agent on the phone to schedule her trip to the west coast. She got *so* upset. He couldn't hear her, because what she was doing spoke so loudly. Immediately she felt pressured, and told him she would call him back.

She called and told me the story, boiling over with frustration. "Can you believe him? He had the nerve to call me with his travel agent, to set-up travel arrangements for this trip. He's crazzz-"

I interrupted her. "He had every right to think that it was OK to plan this trip, because you told him you cared, you told him that you would come to see him and you gave him false hope. It's not him, it's you. You tell him one thing when you mean another."

He can't hear you because what you're doing speaks so loudly.

(Poem) I Am
I Will Never Leave Your Side...

I Am Your God
I Am Your Angel
I Am Your Comforter
I Will Never Leave Your Side
I AM

Your Father
I Am Your Mother
I Am Your Brother
I Am Your Sister
I Will Never Leave Your Side
I AM

Your Husband
I Am Your Wife
I Am Your Lover
I Am Your Mistress
I Am Your Friend
I Will Never Leave Your Side
I AM

Your Need
I Am Your Desire
I Am Your Hope
I Am Your Want
I Will Never Leave Your Side
I AM

Your Strength
I Am Your Stability
I Am Your Joy
I Am Your Peace
I Will Never Leave Your Side
I AM

Your Anything
I Am Your Everything
I Am Your Sure thing
I Will Never Leave Your Side
I AM

Your lift when you are down
I Am Your decision at the fork in the road
I Am Your will to go on
I Will Never Leave Your Side
I AM

Your shout Hallelujah
I Am Your clap for joy
I Am Your dance of praise
I Will Never Leave Your Side
I AM

Your sun when you are cold
I Am Your shelter when you are homeless
I Am Your moon when its dark
I Will Never Leave Your Side
I AM
        I AM
                I AM

YOUR ROCK

Author: Terry Smith

Chapter 11

Letting Go

Letting go is really hard to do, especially if there was Discipline of Intimacy and Communication between the two of you. You loved that person and you feel that you gave the relationship your all. When you really love a person, and for some reason or another the union doesn't work out, there's a knot in the pit of your stomach. Your knees can't seem to support your weight like they did yesterday. Your appetite changes. You can't eat anything or worse- your symptoms are the extreme opposite. You desire nothing but food. Now, that's just cruel. You wonder, "Why is life so unfair?" Just yesterday, life was so lovely.

If you weren't the initiator, but a forced participant in an unpleasant break-up, it's even more difficult. You begin asking yourself one-word questions, "Why?" Why couldn't they see how much I loved them? Why couldn't they love me more? Why can't I have another chance?

I remember a relationship a woman told me about, who attended one of my Teaching the Discipline of Intimacy and Communication, (Teaching the D.I.C.) seminars. I was speaking on "Letting Go" of everything in life that is stopping you from existing at the level you were meant to reach. She stood up and shared her testimony of a relationship that she went through, which ended with her being a forced participant in the break-up. She started out with a vivid comparison, that told just how bad it had hurt her. She would rather have a bikini waxing while in labor, and her eyebrows plucked all at the same time, than feel that pain ever again.

It was a 5-year plus, relationship. They had good D.I.C., were the best of friends and true lovers. You'd think with a combination like that, they were destined for a lifetime of bliss and everlasting happiness. Not so. Five years into the relationship he received an offer for a promotion from his employer. The offer allowed him to stay in his present city, or move to the corporate office that was located on another coast. She surprised him with a party to celebrate his promotion inviting his friends, family and co-workers. After the celebration, they sat down to what she thought was going to be a discussion of the benefits this position offered him. Not what options the promotion offered.

He started out by saying that the company wanted him to move to the corporate office. She said "It's my understanding that with this position, you have the option of staying here." "Yes, but I think it's a wise career move, for me to transfer to the corporate office", he said. Her heart dropped. Waiting for him to mention the obvious, she said "Let's think about all of the pros and cons." He immediately said, with no hesitation "The only con would be if you weren't with me." Good save. That picked her heart up. She had her own business at the time and its success centered on the city where they lived. After seven years of struggling, the business had been going strong for three years and looked to get stronger. "I can't leave. What about the business and all the hard work that I put into it, and all the people that are counting on me for jobs?" she asked him. "You can start a business there and it won't take long for it to be a success, because you know the short cuts this time around", he replied. "You can always stay here", she countered. "This is a great opportunity and I feel I should do this. I should go and you should go with me". Needless to say, he left and she didn't go with him. You probably figured that out. This chapter isn't called "Letting Go" for nothing!

Another five years have passed, and she still struggles with letting go. You see, they stayed together in a long distance relationship. They saw each other every holiday, vacation and for a few unplanned weekends. A distant relationship wasn't easy, but because of their love, they made it work. Right up until the day her world was torn apart. It happened during their second Christmas, as long distance lovers. It was on a Thursday night. She was expecting him to walk through the door at nine. They had planned to decorate the tree together. That was a tradition they'd shared from the first year they were together. And keeping with traditions was important, since they made a promise that nothing would change in their relationship except that their love would grow. By ten-thirty at night she started getting a little concerned. She called the airlines to see if his flight had arrived and had it been on time. Maybe he had stopped to pick-up some things on the way. She called his cell phone, office, and home but no answer. So she started spreading out the tree lights across the floor and unwrapping the ornaments. By midnight her uneasy feeling turned to "he could at least give me a courtesy call". At 1:00 am in the morning, with the phone remaining silent, she went to bed. It was a strange night. She tossed and turned nonstop. The restlessness was as if something inside her would not let her sleep, as if she needed to be up doing something. The next morning she got up and got a glass of orange juice then sat down to call him again. She called his home, office, and cell phone. This time there was an answer. There was a woman's voice on the other end of his cell phone. She said, "Hello, who is this?" "This is Lieutenant Johnson of the Grande County Sheriff's Office," the voice at the other end responded. "Are you related to a Mr. Jones?" "Yes... I am," for one second thinking that the reason that he didn't come home is because he was in jail. Then the soft voice coming from so far away said "Ma'am, I am sorry to inform you there was a serious car accident last night and Mr. Jones was killed instantly".

She was a forced participant in this break-up. Oh yeah... she got engaged that Christmas. She later found out that he was in a hurry to catch his flight and was speeding, because he stopped by the jewelers to pickup the engagement ring he planned to surprise her with on Christmas. She went through anger, depression, guilt, and loneliness. Once she passed through all those stages, just to make sure she did them right, she went through them again. Eventually, she realized she needed to let go and move on.

When you love someone with every fiber of your being, it is hard to let go because of the pain- that pain that you get deep down in the pit of your stomach. Why did our Maker give us this pain?

If you move on to the next relationship too soon, you are overly cautious, and don't give it 100 percent of yourself for fear of feeling the pain again.

To properly let go of our relationships when they end, it is important to ask ourselves, "What made them end?" "What did I learn from the experience?" Take from your past what you need and disregard the rest.

Chapter 12

You Can Bet on Death, But That's All

You're going to die. That's the one thing in life that you can be sure of without assuming. No, you may not know the day or the hour, but you know that you're going to die someday. Now, if you are someone that believes in life after life, or that you'll return as some beautiful species, then that's all right. Let's just agree that you will leave... and you can bet on that. What do I know for sure? You have to ask questions like this, in order to have good Intimacy and Communication. And you must be disciplined about it. When you grow comfortable with someone, you start assuming what is going to happen. Next, you'll be leaving the door open for heartache caused by confusion. Good D.I.C. is a constant thing.

Everything else in life needs confirmation and/or clarification. You weren't born knowing the day and time, someone gives you confirmation. I still question my birth year, but that's a woman thing. Anyway, you're not born knowing who your parents are, what your name is, what your sex is, or even how to live right. You got confirmation and clarification. In life, we must have confirmation in order to decide what direction we are to take. Without some clarity, we are assuming. I admit there are times in life when confirmation or clarification is impossible to achieve. So we must follow our gut instinct, until we find assurance. We have no control in situations like that. It is completely out of our hands. What I want to talk about is unnecessary assumption. Unnecessary assumptions will lead to worry and you know what they say about worrying: "too much worrying can kill you". Remember the only thing in life you can bet on is that you are going to die. You have a great deal of control when everything assumed is confirmed.

I am sure everyone knows someone who has been like this occasionally- What do you think about this? Do you think I should do that? Do you think I was right or he was right – do you, do you, do you? We know these people and most likely we've *been* those people from time to time. Most often the response is "I don't know, did you ask...?" Their response is "NO" and the "do yous" start once again. "Do you think I should or do you think I shouldn't...?"

A relative of mine is a beautiful girl who almost always has her pick of attractive men. She's educated and has a successful career. But, she has an enormous fear in the area of directness, or giving and receiving. When she calls me I can tell how her relationship(s) are going by her lack of conversation. Whenever things are going great she talks and talks for hours. But when things aren't good she calls me at ungodly hours between 11pm and 7am. When things are going badly for her in a relationship, she will call and start with a greeting and then just hold the phone - and me being familiar with this pattern, will have to jump-start the conversation with *the* question. "What's wrong?" And she will say "Uh, he didn't call." I swear, the routine is the same thing every time. She is so predictable. And so am I. She calls me because I have an available 24-hours a day policy on my phone. And I will listen to her and give her the same response. She will say "He didn't call," and I will respond with "Did you call him?" Then she will say, "I'm not calling him." Or the problem might be "He asked if he could postpone our date because he said he had a meeting - what do you think he meant by that?" This is part of a pattern, and so is my response "What was your answer?" "Obviously, we'll have to postpone our plans," she mutters. Then I say, "It doesn't matter what he meant, other than what he said." Sometimes her rationale is from the gender perspective "He's the man, I'm not going to call him first. He needs to call me first. What do you think?" and I always say, "I think I am not going to assume this with you. You appear to be wondering, and worrying unnecessarily. You could ease your mind by simply asking for confirmation." In her case, all she ever needs to do, if things bother her that much, is pick up the phone. By doing this she can go to the source to get answers to her assumptions. However, she feels "safer" with our routine and the fact that she has her pride.

Another friend has this same fear of confronting the affairs of the heart. She says she has the worst luck with men, but she believes her Mr. Right is due anytime, and doesn't want to miss him. She has a big open door in her heart with a sign over it that reads, "Come and do as you please."

She has always been a "one-man woman". The problem is they were "many-women men". I remember countless scenarios that almost always played out the same. She loved the way he looked, spoke and played the guitar. She would listen over, and over, and over, and over to his voice on the answering machine, then she would force all of her roommates, sisters, friends, co-workers, pastor, and psychotherapist to listen. She also told her psychic, who should have foreseen he wasn't Mr. Right for her - but I guess the per-minute charge was more of an incentive than letting her know that a downfall was in her stars.

Part I: So, You Think You Know Yourself...

She loved to love. But, her love was never returned. Her relationships were built on a foundation of assumption. Due to her fear of clarifying the relationship, and her contentment just to wonder—that he cares, if he cares, how he feels, what he wants, she missed out on the opportunity to find something more lasting, and more satisfying.

She only dates one man at a time, and if that man shows an interest in seeing her on a regular basis, she assumes that his and her feelings are the same. Time after time, I would watch her get hurt. She slept with one man she really loved, but later found out she didn't truly know him. In the beginning they spoke almost everyday. She would go to his house and stay the night at his suggestion, but she would never have sex with him. She came home one morning and said with a glow in her eyes, "I can't take being disappointed anymore. The next time I lay next to him we won't get any sleep." Knowing her conviction and how she feels about relationships, I asked, "Are you two in a committed relationship? Did you ask him if he is involved or sleeping with anyone else? Does he love you?" Her response was "No, but I don't think he's seeing anyone else. We talk everyday for hours and he invites me over to spend the night. And I know he really likes me. He looks at me and tells me I am such a good person." I said "And, that you are."

You can't get blood from a turnip, force a horse to drink water, ad finitum, ad nauseum. You get the point. She slept with him the very next day and on the following day he didn't call, so she called him. There was no answer, so she left a message. Another day went by and she still hadn't heard from him so she called again and this time he answered. She said "Why haven't you called me?" "I've been busy," he said. (She could tell by the shortness of his response, where this was going.) "Busy?" she said. "I want to talk to you about the other night." "The other night?" he replied, "What is there to talk about?" "About us." "What about us?" "What do you mean 'what about us'? We made love." "And?" He said. "And! Is that all you have to say?" "I don't owe you anything just because we had sex." He referred to their consummation as sex, instead of making love. "I didn't make you any promises." "*Jerk!*" click...

Part I: So, You Think You Know Yourself...

She was crying and heartbroken, but it wasn't the first time this had happened. And if she doesn't change the way she validates her relationships, this broken heart won't be her last. Good person or not, all relationships that are validated on assumptions always have the question "will they work or will they not?" looming over them. Know this: anything not confirmed is assumed. So ask yourself- What do I know for sure...?

Part II:

Getting Naked

Chapter 13

The Meat Market

Why do you think some people refer to a nightclub as a "Meat Market"? Meat Market doesn't sound very complimentary. Are you just a piece of meat on display until someone chooses you? Can they just trim off the unwanted parts, tenderize, sauté and serve you up? No, if that were the case it would be called The Gourmet Market. Now, some people do display themselves as the daily special in the meat section at the Piggly Wiggly. But the definition of meat, is the flesh of an animal used as food that's edible – the fleshy inner part, the essential part, the core. I mean really think about it... the purpose of going to the meat market for most people is to find someone to hunt, kill, skin, cook and devour. Then you burp, and toss out the leftovers.

Let me share with you, my personal feelings about "The Meat Market". Frequently called a nightclub or *the* spot, it's the only place other than the beach where you try to bare all, for all to see. It is a superficial atmosphere, with superficial people. Oh, there might be many people in a nightclub with substance, the material kind or the personal kind, but it's hard to distinguish between who has substance and who doesn't, because it isn't a requirement to get in the door. You don't have to show your social status card, Noble prize, or Heisman trophy. You don't have to be a scholar or a brain surgeon. Usually, all it takes is cash, borderline dress code or a homey hook-up.

Do you really think you would be happy meeting your mate in a nightclub? The word night doesn't even have a positive definition. Night - the time between dusk and dawn, a time of gloom, obscurity, ignorance, or sadness. You are sure to find ignorance and sadness in a nightclub. The definition of a club- a group of persons organized together for a common purpose. So rightfully, a nightclub is where people come together to indulge in gloom, obscurity, ignorance, and sadness. There is power in knowing that what you're seeing has a shallow surface, no depth underneath, and is unlikely to foster any sense of permanence.

Most of the time, a nightclub is not an organized place. The majority of people have their individual reasons for being there, and are following their own agendas. It is simply an establishment offering drinks, entertainment, and occasionally food. You're sure to find entertainment here and I don't mean the music or the band. Sometimes the entertainers are just the people.

If you've been going to the meat market to find a mate and a little entertainment, try a setting with more intimacy, like an evening hosted at home, for friends and co-workers who are also at "loose ends". Have a party where every single woman has to bring a single girlfriend, and every single man has to bring a single guy friend. That's a good way to start. No matter whom you meet, you already have one thing in common - you are both single. Play interactive games with men versus the women, the dating game, or have a raffle where people can win a date for the day, and donate the proceeds to your favorite charity.

In a more controlled environment there is a better chance of finding out who you have more in common with. Even if you don't get that flutter in the pit of your stomach or your heart doesn't skip a beat, you can still have fun... Try it. This unconditional approach is a much more relaxing and rewarding setting than the Meat Market.

Chapter 14

Truth and Consequences

Men: what is it that tells you which woman will accept the fact that you're married, and which one won't? Over the years, I have posed that question to hundreds of men. The majority admit it's easy to tell the difference between a woman that is lonely and desperate to find a man, even a married one, as opposed to the woman who is relaxed and happy, with or without a man for that night. She is willing to wait a lifetime to find "her" man, and not someone else's.

Part II: Getting Naked

A word for the ladies who have busy lives and find it hard at times to maintain a healthy relationship... know that some men see you as bait for an unfulfilling and casual fling. If you take the time and effort to have a rewarding and successful career, take time to have a fulfilling relationship. Don't let your career interfere with having good D.I.C. skills. Having D.I.C. is your defense against men that think of you as available for a "good time, not a long time".

While attending a charity dinner, I noticed this handsome man watching me from across the room. He was dressed in a dark Armani suit, a pair of Col' Haan's, and for keeping track of *his* good time, a gold Rolex. His skin was clear, his nails manicured, and he laughed at all the right times. He appeared to be someone very popular, since all eyes seemed to be on him. Just to make sure my suspicions were right, and his eyes were on me, I moved to another room and he followed. I could tell that he was trying to find a moment alone to meet me, but it was difficult. His popularity was understandable. I later found out he was the Mayor of the City. He finally found the opportunity to make his way over to the punch bowl near where I was standing. "Hello, is there anything I can get for you?" he said. I said "Anything"? "Well, maybe not anything. But if you tell me what your request is I will see what I can do", he replied. "Something simple- to never have to pay taxes and a bank in my name," I answered. "Well, I'm sure you're not asking for more than you deserve, so in order to get you a bank in your name I would need to know it", he said. We introduced ourselves and that's when I realized who he was. The pictures that I had seen of him didn't do him justice, but they did show him with a wife and family.

"What kind of work do you do?" he asked, and I told him. "Would you have time to do some volunteer work for me?" This is the Mayor asking me for help. What else was I going to say but, "I don't know how much free time I have but I'm sure there is something I can do." He replied, "Why don't you write down your number and get it to me sometime tonight. I'll have my assistant call you". Seeing another group approaching him, he said, "Let us know if there is anything you need, and I hope you enjoy yourself". Then he walked away.

Later, as the evening was coming to an end, the Mayor was shaking hands and wishing everyone a good night. I walked up to him to say goodnight and it was as if we were telepathic and he knew that my number was in the palm of my hand. He reached for my hand, holding it tight, palmed the paper and smiled. Then casually, as if we'd never met before, he said "I don't believe I got your name." I told him again. "Thank you for coming. Have a good night." His actions seemed a little impersonal, but I put it down to the lineup of people behind me, waiting to shake his hand.

Three days later I received a call from his assistant. She told me the date and time of a meeting I was to attend on behalf of the Mayor. She asked me some personal questions too, including my address, my availability, and clarification of the initials in the front of my name, Miss or Mrs. I wasn't sure whether that was really necessary security stuff, but I guess knowing if I was married or not was valuable information to his project.

Alright... maybe not!

This information also verified that I was single, my address, and my time schedule. I attended the meeting and I realized the time frame of the project they wanted me to work on, would not fit into my schedule. So I had to decline.

A week later, I got a call from the Mayor saying that he was sorry to hear that my time didn't permit me to help with this project, and maybe there would be others. "How about meeting me for lunch?" he asked. I said "OK", thinking to myself that lunch is not a date. This does not mean that he is flirting.

The mind is a wonderful thing. We can let it convince us of anything we want to believe. Sometimes who someone is, or how we perceive their standing in our social and professional lives, can blind us to the "real" person. People have to stop caring so much about a person's status and more about their stature.

The Mayor and I had lunch at an exclusive dining club, where it wasn't unusual to have seated across from you, a man accompanied by a beautiful woman that wasn't his wife. This was my first experience in dealing with the "good ol' boy network."

It wasn't that we were not seen. Many gentlemen came to his table and he introduced me to everyone without hesitation. It was also apparent that I was not his secretary, since we were enjoying a lot of seductive eye contact. There was no evidence of a pen, paper or tape recorder to take dictation and the thought of me passing off as his wife was laughable. Everyone who follows the city news, has seen a picture of " his significant other" in the papers. I heard it said once, "The thrill is in the hunt (me) not the kill (wife)." When his eyes weren't looking into mine, they never moved further away than the second snap of my suit that was secured only by a shiny silver fastener. It appeared that if I inhaled too deeply, the snap would open and expose my breast. The hunt was on!

You really have to admire that good ol' boy network of the city's most powerful men in their private club, seated at tables with women that weren't their own. If women themselves operated in this same manner, to see and not see, to know, but never speak of it- a universal motto, they could also enjoy the pleasure of exclusive clubs like this.

During lunch, we talked about my family and his. He mostly spoke about his kids. I asked how the project was going, only to fill a lull in the conversation. He said, "Everything is going fine with that". Then he asked if I was involved with anyone seriously. I told him no, I am just dating. He smiled and said,

"I'm sure you are a woman of many choices". I smiled, hoping the broccoli I was eating wasn't sticking between my teeth. We finished lunch. He had to get back to work and I wasn't quite sure where to go from there. He asked if he could call me later and I said "Sure." It was hardly out of my mouth, before I was asking myself, why did I say "sure"? Why did he ask if he could call me? What did we have in common? He knew that I did not have time to help with his project. What does he really want and where is this going? I didn't hear from him that night, but within a couple of days, I received a call from his assistant inviting me to a private party. Each guest needed a ticket, including me, and anyone that I wanted to invite. She asked, "How many tickets would you need?" I hesitated and said "Two". She said, "I will send you three." Later, I realized that by requesting two tickets, I gave the impression that I might bring a date. I assumed her response was to clue me in, that when the Mayor invites me to a private party, he doesn't mean for me to bring a date. Instead, I should bring "attractive girlfriends". This was just an assumption.

Part II: Getting Naked

So of course, I invited two of my girlfriends. When we arrived at the party we found out it was in honor of a man that had done something great for the city, but that's all I remember. I really wasn't paying much attention to the reason for the party. All I knew was that the Mayor was there and he was looking good. He noticed me when I entered the room. He greeted me with that political greeting. You know... the usual "Thanks for coming, glad you could make it", line. They say this while they are looking over your head or to the side of you, then they move on to the next prospective voter.

My girlfriends and I attended another party a couple of weeks later given by a National Organization. I noticed something strange happening. Men were coming up to me saying "hello" and addressing me by my name. Men that I was sure I had never met before. With almost every step I made, some strange man would greet me by name. I told my girlfriend, "I have to get out of here... this is too weird."

The first time I met the Mayor, at that private gathering, my hair was brown. Some time later, after I had changed my hair color, I went to a function that had nothing to do with politics or the Mayor. Just a nice night out with some friends. The next time the Mayor called me, he said, "So you changed your hair color". I asked how he knew that, since *I* knew he wasn't at the party. He replied, "I know a lot. I have my ways."

Well, I guess that pulls the cork on the theory that only you and your hairdresser will know. This was weird. He didn't even come to the party. I was not a member of the host's organization, so my name wasn't on a list and no one knew that I was attending, before I decided to go that day. So, it was no mystery- the word was out that I was connected to the Mayor somehow. This was something I didn't like. I mean come on... it's a woman's prerogative to change her hair color and not make my hair color the city's business!

Then a close male friend gave me a lesson in Lust Networking 101. The way things work...if someone (good ol' boy) is interested in someone (me), he discretely lets his interest be known amongst his peers. Then the name of the Hunted party (me) is passed around and becomes off-limits.

I know the person of interest was the Mayor, but what gives any of them the right to label me off -limits? After the "hair"

Part II: Getting Naked

conversation, I wanted no part of this world. I kept my distance and refrained from attending any political functions or good ol' boy parties.

The Mayor called one day and said that since he was in the neighborhood, could he stop by for a visit? I said, "Yes, you are welcome." I began to give him directions to my house when he interrupted me. "I know exactly where it is. I should be there in ten minutes or less." Everything in my mind seemed to stop except for those words "I know exactly where it is," which kept playing over and over. He was still talking when my brain started functioning again. I thought to myself, my house isn't an easy place to find- it's off the main road and down a long widening path. So, in order to drive past my house, you would literally have to be coming it. I heard a dial tone and realized that he had hung up. I believe he said something about ten minutes.

When the bell rang, I answered the door. He hugged me and sat down. I offered him a drink. He declined. At that moment reality hit me- this was the Mayor of the city sitting in my living room without his wife and children, talking in front of me about the people of the city's business.

Today, I truly understand Monica Lewinsky's entanglement. I believe that Bill Clinton knew without a doubt, that Monica would comply with his wishes on how the relationship would be conducted. The Mayor may have had a Clarence Thomas and Bill Clinton mentality, but I wasn't an Anita Hill or Monica Lewinsky. I was determined to let him know that I would not comply with his desires. He would not delegate how this friendship or casual acquaintance would go.

I can be pretty blunt. If I want to know something, I will ask questions. I wanted to know, so I asked. "Being a man in your position", I asked, "How do you know which woman, in a crowded room, you can approach? You have never met this woman and you don't know anything about her. How do you know who is safe to approach, and won't tell your wife?" He laughed and said, "You really want to know?" "Yes", I replied. "Have you got some kind of radar that tells you that this woman is a go, and the other one is not?" He said, "Yes. There are some clues, some signs that you can pick up on, that lets me know which woman would most likely be willing to accept the fact that I am married and will keep our relationship confidential."

Part II: Getting Naked

What clues had I shown him, I wondered, while thinking to myself, 'I could take a picture of this man in my house. I could have a hidden camera pointing at him. I could have called the news media and had them waiting outside my door. How did he know that I wasn't that type? What was it about me, that made him willing to take the chance?' He said "The biggest rule that I, as well as many other married men follow (pay attention ladies this is food for thought), is to never pursue a woman that has only a nine-to-five job and no outside hobbies or activities requiring her time. That's a dangerous situation because if you provide her with enjoyment that fills in her extra time, she will be looking for you every time she has a need for companionship and that will be almost every other day. I don't care how beautiful she is. I will not deal with that type of woman. That's the kind of woman that will call your house".

I'll be damned if the counselor didn't have a modus operandi.

He continued, "But, a woman that has more going on in her life other than just her career- she might have a very hectic schedule, she could own her own business, she could work long hours, she could travel a lot... she has very limited time in her schedule. Her schedule hinders her from having a fully satisfying relationship. Now, this type of woman might be willing to take a limited type of romance as opposed to no romance." He might as well have said, "Getting a little on the side is better than getting none at all to her".

So, be careful of what you ask for, because you might get an answer you never expected. I was amazed at how confident he appeared to be in the analytical way he would approach a woman he was interested in. After that information, I wanted him out of there. So, I told him we were leaving and going to dinner. He said that he would have to go, because he had to take care of a call he'd received. I walked him to the door, thanked him for coming, and said "Goodbye."

I feel it important to explain my reasons for divulging his martial status and political position. That first evening when we met, I was aware that he was the Mayor and a married man. It took no arm- twisting for me to give him my number. But I think it's important that readers of this episode understand this is not just another story of a powerful married man that cheats on his wife with a naive woman. Remember, the underlying theme of this book- "freedom comes from taking ownership of your choices". Even though he is a man in a position of power, it is my decision and choice whether to give in to his will. It was my choice not to be a participant.

Also, my point was to see how you felt reading his (as-well-as other men's) beliefs about women high achievers and women that have a nine to five job and no outside interests without a man. He believes women who work hard, or who have high-powered careers, sacrifice having someone in their bed for life, to what they get from working. A woman that works only nine to five and has no outside hobbies, is thought of as a woman that has too much time on her hands, and will demand that the man in her life, fill it.

Before the release of this book, I asked the proofreaders (twelve of them women) some questions relevant to this chapter. I asked: is the fact that he was the Mayor, an important part of the lesson? Also, what was their understanding of my reason for divulging his martial status and position?

Many of the answers were negative and condemning of male attitudes. That most men of power cheat on their wives and take advantage of naive women, was a common thread. Other responses were: it's important to sensationalize the story or, it helps to reflect on President Bill Clinton's infidelity scandal. None of the responses supported my own rationale.

My reasons had nothing to do with men and their power, but everything to do with the pedestal on which women place powerful men. Most females would not argue with the assertion that powerful men are attractive. Maybe because when we were little girls the superheroes—Batman and Superman, appeared to be so powerful and never failed to rescue their women.

We are attracted to men that take care of us, like our nation's leaders, our male bosses and the most unspoken attraction...our spiritual leader. Unlike other attractions, when it comes down to a married woman catering to her Pastor, she has the support of a husband. The role of pastoral service places a man next to the greatest power of all, God.

We sometimes see men positioned to lead us, as fearless or heroic. He knew that because of his position as Mayor, there were women willing to meet with his wishes. Not because of the man he is, but because of the man women want him to be. Manipulation was effortless for him, because he believes that the women he chooses are happier seeing to his health, welfare and well-being.

Once I heard how he viewed women that worked hard to raise themselves up in life, I knew I couldn't be a victim to his beliefs. From that day on, I never spent any more time alone with him, lunch, dinner or otherwise. We remained distant acquaintances. I have never forgotten his formula for approaching the type of women he thought would be temporarily satisfied, dating a married man.

Chapter 15

The Confident Man's Perspective

Months later, while the conversation I had with the mayor was still fresh in my mind, I decided to ask my step-brother about what the Mayor told me. My brother seems to be successful at playing the field. I can't remember a time when he ever complained about confusion between him and any of his many women. I can't say that he and every woman in his life had good D.I.C., but I am sure that by him being my brother, that mother's words of wisdom were instilled in him as well.

Part II: Getting Naked

I told him what the Mayor said. To my surprise, he disagreed. A confident man who doesn't leave room for indecisiveness, he volunteered to write down his perspective for this chapter of my book.

He believes, that eight out of every ten women are constantly searching for some type of guidance, be it spiritual, professional, or personal. They ultimately want a man, satisfying companionship, or God. And in most cases, the ladies that are seeking God, ask Him to find them a man. Women want a man who has a *program* they can walk into, lay down and feel safe and comfortable in.

Program is defined first by a person's focus, discipline and goal-orientation in life; second by their professional standing, accomplishments and goals; and third by their intellectual horsepower and how well thought out their plans are to achieve their personal and professional goals. For many women, their assessment of a man's "program" determines their assessment of how successful he is. Even the women who have a man with a strong program, are looking for some-one who has a bigger program.

He said, "At one time, I found myself frustrated with how women didn't seem to be put together tightly. Nor did any of them seem to be all of what I wanted—domestic, physically fit, mentally fit, and possessing great time management skills. I later realized that they were what they were meant to be from the beginning of time, a weaker vessel and a Helpmate. I don't say this in a chauvinistic way, but the man's job is to have a plan/program that will include goals and benefits the woman can participate in. If the two solidify the bond between man and woman, and work as God meant them to work, there is nothing they cannot accomplish.

"I realized a long time ago that the best way to attract a woman's interest was to use techniques similar to those in a Martial Art known as "Akido". In Akido it is taught that one should take energy from an oncoming force (offense) and channel it (defense) in a more beneficial direction. Taking a woman with a strong mind and going head to head with her, is to set up a confrontation, or win/lose situation. The optimal thing to do, is to redirect her thinking, giving you the opportunity to influence her actions in a way you find conducive to the relationship, or what I call the program. Guys I know would always talk about how they met a woman, bedded her, and then when they tried to get with her again maybe days, weeks or months later, encountered resistance. Because they simply overrode the niceties for a short-term gain. Very few bothered to invest in a more "profit yielding" approach of enticing, seducing and catering to her every whim and desire.

It is often an advantage to find out what everyone else is doing, and do the opposite. Chivalry is far from dead. Most guys think this technique is corny, or weak. But, when that woman is sitting at home thinking about what they want to do or who they prefer to spend their time with, they remember the conversation, atmosphere and little things you did for them. Yes, sex may be the main course, but it's the little appetizers working up to that dish, that the other guy forgot to put on his menu. Women want to be pampered, cared for and made to feel special. That's what my angle boils down to. Even if you have five women, who may or may not know about each other. When that one woman comes around, they want to be made to feel like it's all about them, for whatever time you are together. That means no phones ringing at one or two in the morning, no hair left on the bathroom floor and no other women's items to be found.

The man's role is to run the house and control the situation at all times, and in most cases at all costs, to protect his program. At times this can call for some manipulation, but this must always be a prerogative that is open to the man. In no way is manipulation to be confused with deception. He is only redirecting actions, thoughts or plans onto another track. This is all done to protect the program.

Chapter 16

The Confident Woman's Rebuttal

OK, ladies. At this point I find it necessary to respond to the last two chapters. In "Truth and Consequences", men state that they can home in on the woman that is lonely and desperate to find a man, and tell them from the woman that is more relaxed and happy with or without a man for that night. In "The Confident Man's Perspective", it's claimed that women want a man who has a *program* they can walk into, lay down and feel safe and comfortable in. I find it hilarious that men think they are being so logical, when it comes down to what women will or won't do, and what they want from men, sex and relationships.

Part II: Getting Naked

Excluding the married or single issues, I agree with some of the basic elements in the Mayor's modus operandi. You can definitely pick up clues from a person's conversation or body language that leads you to think they may agree to see someone, even if they're not single. If you are good at reading body language, sometimes the clues are so strong that there is little doubt whether or not a person will, or won't agree to "deal" with someone that isn't available. Sure... it's a deal arrangement or agreement most definitely! Adultery is an open secret, in America. I don't admire, condone, or support adultery. That's not what this rebuttal is about.

The world's most famous adultery scandals are a "who's who" of the political and the powerful, including Jesse Jackson, and President J.F. Kennedy (and many another Kennedy for that matter). When you whisper the words "adultery" and "scandal", no example is more famous than the one involving President Bill Clinton and his unfortunate partner, Monica Lewinsky. This scandal, if none other, proved that adultery is here to stay. Bill Clinton remained our nation's leader. Few people were disappointed or surprised. Some responses to the openly acknowledged adultery were, "He's a good President, and if he needed a little on the side, it's okay as long as he can run the nation." There was more anger over the money spent to investigate something that was a known fact. It was known while he was campaigning for his first term, that he may have had extramarital relationships. What was surprising, was that many people were upset about the type of women with whom he chose to commit adultery. Perhaps it would have been more palatable, if the affair had been with someone of Marilyn Monroe's status and stature. Many politicians have affairs. I would say a conservative estimate is 35% of them. How many of those pointing the finger at Clinton, could have been tarred with the same brush? The trial was not about Lewinsky. It had a lot of other agendas attached to it. The country followed along, without noticing that some events directly affected them.

Adulterers do not need endorsers. Infidelity is a disease that is caused by very poor D.I.C.

When two people get together, and one or neither is single, the understanding is that they are going to negotiate and come to terms about their relationship (cheating). Then a deal is made with contingency clauses between the agreeing parties. Some people actually verbalize the agreement. This is business- I agree to do this if you agree to do that—If you take care of me, I'll take care of you. In layman's terms, if you "keep providing, I'll keep a riding". Let's not forget the famous line in one of Tina Tuner's big hits, "What's Love Got To Do With It?" In some relationships, I agree, love has *nothing* to do with it. Because loyalty/discipline, understanding/communication, and trust/intimacy have every-thing to do with the beginning of a good relationship, not this made- up, over-publicized thing called "love." Love, by its own definition, is an extra bonus to the person who has good D.I.C.

I agree with the Mayor's point that how active a person is, determines the amount of time they want from you in that relationship. In my experience while dating, I find the men who have demanding careers (Doctors, Attorneys, CEO's) are very appreciative of the small intimate surprises that take little to no effort on my part (teddy, honey, whip cream, etc.). I believe it's because their schedule is so full, and they are responsible for giving to so many, that when someone gives them something that is unconditional and is not related to the business at hand, the gesture is valued more. Understanding them in this way, has allowed me to get a great deal more out of my relationships emotionally. It's different for the man whose career is less demanding, more normal or who, to quote the Mayor, "has only a nine to five and no outside hobbies or activities" requiring his attention. Maybe because there *is* less demand of his time, he and his significant other, are able to indulge in timeless, pleasurable enjoyment and intimacy. If you provide him with the pleasurable enjoyment that he needs to fill in his extra time, you have a good chance of being the one he chooses to continue to satisfy his deal.

Sex can be the same. In dealing with people that desire companionship, no matter the gender, the one who provides pleasure and enjoyment is the one they will usually want to continue seeing.

The difference here, is if a man wants his needs filled and you are the one picked to oblige, then he will look for you to continue providing him with pleasurable moments that fill up his extra time. This is *my* opinion, from my experience in dealing with men. On the other hand, if you provide a woman with pleasurable enjoyment that fills in her extra time, she will want you to please her wish for companionship.

From my experience and perspective about women, there are also relationships based strictly on an exchange of goods or services, between a man and a woman. The women that are involved in this type of relationship, are there to provide companionship and romance in exchange for financial, material or personal satisfaction. Most often the attraction is the woman's youth and beauty, to men that may even be their father's age, but who make a salary with considerably more zeros than their parent. They are considered eye candy and they know it. They have the ability to manipulate a man's mind in a way they find conducive to the relationship, or what they consider part of the "program," to quote "The Confident Man's Perspective". These women have a remarkable way of making him believe as though she feels fortunate to be with a fine specimen of manhood, such as himself. All while never losing sight of the fact that they are with this man for personal gain. Let the chips fall where they may. It doesn't matter if they are the second or third concubine, or the spouse, as long as the money, mortgage and vacations are available.

Men are creatures that conquer and devour. If the sport is not challenging, it's not interesting. Your paying for half is not going to get you any more points than the woman that rides free. Some men seem to get an extra notch on their macho belt, when they have a "trophy" woman on their arm. This kind of man knows that he must keep her pleased with things that cannot be secured with the average income. He is always aware that his big toys are what attract her. They are his security. He also knows that no matter how far they go, he can only be replaced by with men with bigger toys. For women who are in a relationship where they exchange their looks for financial, monetary or personal satisfaction, it's not about love. It's about understanding the deal. "If you are willing to pay, you can play." Men pay out of their wallets. Women pay out of their selves.

Some men take pride in being able to play because they can afford to pay. The conquest is about the competitiveness inside them, which at the end of the game gets them the trophy. These are the type of men who would not date the independent

Part II: Getting Naked

girl or should I say the girl that is willing to do her part, pay her share of the bills, or go Dutch treat. She's not challenging for him -- even though she could love him without the toys (Jennifer Lopez puts it well in "Love Don't Cost A Thing"). He's not interested in her -- he'd label her too easy.

Chapter 17

Interview Yourself

I interviewed a group of ten single women for this book. The topic of discussion was "What makes a good mate?" Somehow, with this group of women, I wasn't surprised that no one mentioned having good D.I.C. skills. Seven out of ten preferred a man that could provide for them, but they were willing to help if it appeared the ship were sinking, however that was a big "but." If they had a choice, they wanted a man that could perform miracles and find his own way to save the ship. Two out of the remaining three, were looking for a man that wanted a woman to stay home, take care of the house and keep them happy. That was all. One out of the ten had a problem with women that expected men to take care of them. She said, and I quote "I think women that are looking for men to provide for them while they do nothing, are just being a bitch". When I heard this, I thought of a great line from a book called "Delores Claiborne" by Steven King. The line was, "sometimes being a bitch is all a woman has to hang onto". Once she made the statement that she didn't need a man to take care of her, the karma in the room changed. I immediately felt as if I knew what the other women were thinking. The woman who made that statement, was the least attractive of the group. I could hear the other women's minds working-'Well, it's understandable... look at her. She does not have as many choices as we do.' I asked her why she felt this way in a society that rears men to be conquerors and providers, and where, for the most part, women are taught to follow and to wait for someone to provide for them. She told us a story of how she had dated a man that she wanted to marry. He didn't have much money, but she asked him to marry her, because she was okay with being an equal provider. She even bought him an engagement ring. The relationship didn't work out and when they later broke up, he kept the ring.

One of the ladies asked her why they had broken up. She said she found out that he was cheating on her. He chose to be with the other women and so he left her. I heard one of the other women say, "Honey, if a man is going to drive you crazy, at least have one that can afford your counseling". Amen!

I then asked a second group, the same question- "What makes a good mate?" This group consisted of both men and women. This time I used the Internet as my medium. These are the responses I got back, presented exactly as they were received.

Some things that make a good mate:

Honesty, trust, and just the ability to be yourself
Someone who you can trust with your inner most secrets and thoughts. Someone who is there for you in the good times and the bad, they cherish each other's hopes and are kind to each other's dreams, he warms my presence, remembers me in his prayers, he is there to listen and care about the feelings that we share!

What I look for in a man is honesty, someone I can trust and believe in.

A woman that will stay with me no matter what type of times I am going through. Someone that I can tell my most inner thoughts to and have confidence that she will not tell the world. A woman that no matter what I do, she is by my side and will stand strong with me.

Part II: Getting Naked

Someone that shows mutual respect, understanding and accepting each other's differences and similarities. Someone that has a sense of humor, looking beyond a friend's circumstance and sees their potential.

I look for honesty in a mate. Someone you can rely on and accepts you for who you are.

Relationships are based on loyalty, honesty and unconditional love.

Hopefully this will help!

Initially I would say that I look for women with similar likes and dislikes. But, through my experience in growing up I find that most of my romantic relationships have ended up being women that I initially did not like but admired. With all of that considered, I find that some things I look for in a mate is honesty, good listener, not judgmental, self motivated.

A man with depth, and empathy. It's very important for me to find a mate that believes in his own self-improvement.

What makes a good mate to me is a woman that can be honest. A woman that has a positive attitude, common sense, courtesy with other people and that is open-minded.

All of the responses I received were along the lines of what I expected-- truth, honesty, and someone that person could communicate with. However, I've underlined one because this response struck me as being so profound.

150

Other then the fact that the first group consisted of all women and the second both men/women, why were the responses to the same question so different? My theory is that as women, we sometimes measure the quality of other women's mates by what they can provide for their significant other. So when women are in a group and they are discussing "What makes a good mate?" It's like a competition to want someone that can provide the most "things". In reality someone that has good D.I.C. is what we want most.

The threat of competition was removed and the question was asked to the second group, which consisted of both men and women via the Internet. The answers from both genders were about the need for compatibility, familiarity and feelings, not things.

Some friends we now like, and have grown to love, were originally people whom we never dreamed we would get along with. Only after we were given the opportunity to get to know them better, and were able to add depth to a relationship that was shallow in its beginning, did we find that we had a great deal in common.

Part II: Getting Naked

I believe my point is clear without having to write one word more. If I were to ask you, which of the girls in answering the previous question appeared to be the most shallow, you would probably say, the not-so-attractive one. The truth is they all are. Each one of their statements lacked emotional depth. They looked for someone to provide them with the material things that make a relationship little more than superficial. At what point in our lives did so many of us decide that friendship qualities were not the most important things we should look for in an intimate relationship? It's as if we don't give a damn about our sanity, and that we'd rather sacrifice the peace that comes from "D.I.C." for temporary satisfaction.

Chapter 18

When Is Hearing "I'm Sorry" Enough?

His daily ritual is to encourage you not to care about yourself by magnifying your low self-esteem. He is frequently saying how worthless you are, and never misses the opportunity to emphasize your good fortune when he chose you over others. Once he finishes breaking your spirit, he tells you he's sorry. Having discouraged all positive thoughts of "I can" by reminding you that you are hopeless, he goes on to say he loves you anyway.

Time after time this happens, and you remember how he had his male dominance issues when you were dating, but wasn't as bad as this.

Part III: How You Like *You* Now?

Since you are a homemaker, you're expected to be at home during the day. Being there, affords you the opportunity to nurture the kids and have a warm welcome and wonderful dinner waiting, when he comes home from his demanding job. It's only right that on the weekend you should also be the one to keep the kids occupied, so he can have time to himself. Time to watch the game, golf, or so he can do the things of his choice. Because as he says, "I'm sorry but you have the luxury of staying at home all day." Which means of course, that you had all that "free" time to do what you want. Oh yes, let's not forget that he loves you.

He tells you about business dinners that his partner's wives were invited to, but not you, because you wouldn't have fit in. His reason is, because of his hard work the only thing you do all day is sit at home, so you wouldn't have anything worth discussing. I guess the one good thing about his hard work is that he oftentimes works late, which allows you some opportunity to chat with your best friend. What's strange is, that on most nights he works overtime, you can't find her. No worry. She is a good friend.

When is hearing "I'm Sorry" enough? The answer is, when your heart and your mind are in sync with one another. If a person keeps saying, "I'm sorry", yet continues to keep doing the same thing and you keep accepting the apology, what will "stop" them from disappointing you again? Why does your heart continue wanting to believe that things will be different this time, even when your mind tells you that it's not going to change?

"That's why I love you like I do. Though you do me like you do..." (Betty Wright, After The Pain)

Those who have been in unfaithful relationships, may have found yourselves wondering why "sorry" was enough to make you stay, in the same way women remain in physically abusive relationships. What makes us want to spend time around people that lie and hurt the very ones they confess to love? Why do victims continue to allow themselves to be singled out for persecution by shallow people, without any substance or depth? Remember: association brings on assimilation.

Some victims fall into a "shallow" world after a tragic event in their lives. They are then vulnerable, and open to almost any companionship for solace. More often then not, these are the people with bad D.I.C. skills.

Some victimizers are going, or have gone through something terrible in their own lives, and as long as you are not being abused it's understandable if you want to believe that this, or the next "sorry", will be the last. Unfortunately some people lie, cheat and thrive on deceiving others. They have no tragic experience to blame their behavior on. They are just being themselves. Some of us have experienced this. Some have become so engulfed in relationships with little depth, that our health and lives are affected by continuing to care for someone who couldn't care less about us.

We know fire is hot so we stay away from it, to avoid being burned. We know that knives cut, so we are careful with them.

And we know that "Sorry" is not always "Sorry, It Won't Happen Again" but we take that chance. Some of us were taught in church, that faith is the foundation on which we hope, and that having faith can grant what me need most. We don't want to give up too soon because this "Sorry" could be the last, and things could get better. It's like playing the slot machines in Vegas. If you walk away too soon, someone comes along and gets your winnings and the winnings only took one more coin.

You know someone who continues to keep going back into the same bad relationship and you wonder to yourself, "When are they going to get tired of living like that?" You give them advice, they listen and later choose to ignore your suggestion and continue on the way they were. Is the nightmare ever going to end?

Someone says time and time again that they will call you and they don't. You tell them that it bothers you when they don't keep their word and the response is always "I'm Sorry". *When* is being sick-and-tired, of being sick-and-tired, ever going to be enough? If they say this is the last time they will ever cheat and

Part III: How You Like *You* Now?

that they are "sorry" about the other times -- will this time be enough?

"Enough!" That time comes, when your heart tells you it is tired of being hurt and your mind is fed up with being troubled. That's when, "Sorry", "Sorry", "Sorry Is Enough!"

Part III:

How You Like *You* Now?

(Poem) Intimacy
You Say You Have Me

You say you have me... You abused me
You say you have me... You misused me
You say you have me... You misunderstood me
You say you have me... You used me to gain
You say you have me... You made me hurt
You say you have me... You used me for all the perks

You say you have me but you don't
You, You, and you don't have me... and neither do you

      Tell me how...
              Huh?
    Tell me now!
              You say you want to have me?

Part III: How You Like *You* Now?

Listen...
It takes patience, kindness, wellness,
wanting and drive

When *you* can say to another...

I know your joy
I know your laugh
I know your smell
I know your touch

I know your troubles
I know your pain
I know your fear of everything

I know the salt of your tears
I know your thoughts

I know which ear to nibble
I know which breast to crest
I know your breath of ecstasy

I know every curve on your perfect body

This is when you know you have me—*Intimacy*

Chapter 19

Sex and Lovemaking Are Two Different Acts

"Let's talk about sex, baby". When the trio, Salt-N-Pepa, first vocalized those words in their hit song titled "Let's Talk About Sex", the lyrics caused a frenzy. The group's daring, expressed how significant it is to talk openly about sex. The song was done at the height of AIDS awareness, but focused on the younger generation's sexual experimentation. No other music groups had dared to speak so candidly about sex to their younger fans. Some thought of the lyrics as an invitation for young people to have sex. Later, the trio was applauded for bringing out a song that caused not only the young, but all people to take a look at how they communicate about sex, lovemaking and intimacy.

Its been said that sex and lovemaking are two different acts. Are they really? Sex can be a selfish activity. Sometimes the goal is to gain power, get money, or to quote the younger generation "just to get the booty". The word "lovemaking" means sexual activity, especially intercourse. Lovemaking is thought of as a selfless act because most of the time the act is between two people that are in a courtship. The goal is to give fulfillment, to satisfy, to give pleasure until the "booty" is satisfied.

Courtship or not, the goal is to reach a state of physical excitement, ecstasy and euphoria. If we're lucky, this is what the first sexual experience is like. Most of us aren't that fortunate because sex is not always a pleasurable experience. Your mood, mind, and heart play a big part in what you receive from the encounter.

There are some people who have never enjoyed sexual intercourse, and have committed themselves to abstinence. They tried sex and then for different reasons they come to the conclusion that intercourse is not for them. And of course there are the few that enjoy sex so much, that it doesn't matter who you are—race, color, religion or gender, if you are "available", you'll do. Excluding these few, let me talk about the people in the middle.

When the relationship, situation, circumstances and surroundings are right, most people will enjoy making love or having sexual intercourse. Lovemaking is a beautiful activity when the couple who are involved, agree that it's not the sex that's keeping them together. Once the lust has been tamped down a few degrees, the passion feels good. You're able to see your significant other without the smoke of sexual tension, and there's a warm sensation that keeps you feeling good about your choice. It's like an old shoe... you know that it's going to look, feel and fit just right.

Sex can take you to a heightened state of mind and body. It can become addictive. Too many people make the mistake of thinking that it was love that made someone want to have sex with them. The escapade wasn't love, it was lust and the act—

just sex. Making love can be so beautiful, pleasing, gentle and patient. When you are making love with someone and your heart and your emotions are sensing that this is the one, it's such a beautiful feeling. You may not experience the feeling every time you are making love to this person, but in your heart there's that feeling of intimacy, courtship, and love. That's lovemaking.

Sex is a selfish act. It's often accomplished simply to experience physical pleasure. The satisfaction that comes from the physical sensations is alright, as long as you acknowledge that it's just sex. There are those who decide not to have sexual intercourse until it's the "right time"... but for whom? If you know that you are eventually going to have sex with a man, what difference does a day make, if you're not holding out until you are in love? If you're not in love with the guy and your purpose for holding out is because you hope he'll think of you as a more respectable person, then waiting is in vain. If you have not practiced good D.I.C. throughout those hold-out days, what difference will 24 hours make? It's still sex without any D.I.C.

It's different if your goal is to be in love, in a committed relationship, before experiencing sexual intercourse. You're waiting until there is intimacy and good communication. Even in a long-term relationship, you can still enjoy the sex. The frolic can be just as enjoyable, euphoric and feel like it's just a romp for one mischievous night, as when you first became a couple. With a courtship, there is one added bonus. After the sex is over, there is still love, but more importantly, genuine "like".

Someone can treat you like a queen, have sex with you and not love or like you. Sex has been used as a barter system since the beginning of mankind. The exchange of affection for affection, money, goods, etc. was, and still is, being made. Some feel that if they do it "right", and often enough, (even if they don't want too) they can stop the partner they are having sex with, from turning to another person for gratification. You may not be having sex with someone for money, but you are trading sex for a sense of security that can't be "bought" any other way. It's a superficial desire, having nothing to do with the pleasure of being held, touched or your needs met. That's wrong!

Part III: How You Like *You* Now?

One way to make certain that your wishes are understood, is to have a dating contract prepared for the suitor to sign before going out. It's a tool that has many uses in this day and age. The contract can say anything that you wish, and in anyway you wish to say it. Some dating contracts state that the applicant for your company agrees not to suggest sex, and if their feelings should change, that a discussion will happen before anything is taken for granted. This may sound unusual, but a written contract is a way to communicate your wishes from the start. Having a clear understanding, shows common sense and good D.I.C. skills.

Chapter 20

Digging Deeper: To The Bone...

Dig deeper to find someone that really enjoys you. Take your time to enjoy the journey towards a relationship. This is when a friendship can develop. Sometimes a successful search takes digging beyond the top layers, to find the treasure underneath.

Example: I have girlfriends in relationships, who shine like a coin being lovingly polished, when they talk about their mates. Their faces light up, and as I look at them sharing cherished thoughts, it's obvious that they and their special someone are spending time nurturing, encouraging, developing, and polishing the relationship. That's why these women shine and that is a good thing.

"When preparation meets opportunity, success comes." This is an excellent quote to build the foundation of a relationship on.

Have you ever been in a position where you felt as if you were paying a debt to society by taking on a charity case? You had more going for yourself, than the person you were dating, did.

If you think that you're dating someone who is below "your" standards, you are shallow. Granted, I believe that we should find someone that we are attracted to on the outside, but "lust" first for what's on the inside. Dig deeper to find how someone communicates, and between the two of you, look for the intimacy.

Find what you are seeking, through the windows of their soul (their eyes). I believe that people's eyes can sometimes speak to you, by showing that the person is honest, lying, sad, or happy. The next time that you have "stopped" to communicate with someone special, listen to what his or her eyes are saying.

It's wonderful that someone thought enough of you to be willing to spend time together. Don't look at this opportunity as if you are doing them a favor, because sometimes these are the types of people we can never get out of our mind, and we will always wonder why they left us as opposed to us leaving them.

A person who you think of as below "your" standards, may have more confidence and ability in themselves, than you do. For example, you may need others to tell you that you're somebody, while the person you consider below your standards, may be more self-assured. You may need others to tell you that you are pretty, (My mother says "Pretty is on the outside, where beauty is skin deep. But ugly is to the bone".) when "pretty" on the inside, is more important to your sub-standard date. You may need others to tell you how successful you are, where a self-assured person knows that success is measured on an individual basis. We don't like to give credit to individuals we perceive as below our standards. However, the good thing about them is that they work on their own credit. They are happy just being the icing on their own cake. I must admit, I like these kinds of people. They lay their expectations of you on the line. They are happy with themselves and they aren't looking to change. There's nothing at all wrong with that. They matter in their life and they know it.

I love confident people, which is not to be confused with conceited people. The confident are happy with themselves, not in the things that they have, and are in love with life itself. They're living high on being alive. They're happy with the little things- the fact that they have a roof over their head, a job to go to, clothes on their back and they are able to share those things with others. When the sun comes up, or the stars show in the sky at night it's an event. Most of all, they take responsibility for the things that happen in their life, the things they have control over. They don't put blame on others where blame should not be. Discernment is a gift they are acutely aware of, knowing right from wrong by instinct, and believing that they should be held accountable for what they do wrong in life. They're not the ones that sit around and have pity parties over what others have done, or what they didn't get out of life. Their parents aren't vilified for not having given them all of life's trinkets. When you talk to them, they're always happy. They don't complain about their day at work, every little ailment, or the things they do not have. I'm sure everyone knows at least one person, who every time you speak to him or her, has a complaint about something going on in their life.

One of my high school classmates comes from a family of blue bloods and royalty. How do I know this was true? Because she told us. I once had an elementary school classmate that had a black belt in karate. How do I know? Because, she told us. Rumor: that her family was rich, and her Dad was some big shot where he worked. All I know to be *true*, was that her mother was one of a small number of stay-at-home wives and mothers, and her dad was a VP at a coastline company. Her mother was beautiful. She didn't look like the other mom's, except for mine (nice save mom, right...wink). She was amazingly nice and smelled like a garden of flowers. She reminded me of Florence Henderson on "The Brady Bunch".

Their house was always so clean, it looked like they never lived there. It was in an upper-class neighborhood... nice yard, cars, a lot of clubs, garden, bridge, and country. Most of the mothers in this neighborhood didn't work. I remember praying that one day we could move there, because I knew my mother was tired of working two jobs so we could have things that we needed.

There was no doubt that my classmate got her looks from her mother. If she'd been born a man, she would have been a dashing specimen, like her dad. She was the captain of the varsity cheerleading squad, president of the yearbook club, and homecoming queen (junior *and* senior year). Her peers worshiped, envied and voted her best looking in the yearbook. None of her friends, or should I say followers, (yes, I was one of them) were equal to her, by her standards. We weren't as pretty, popular, or hadn't received a fancy car for our 17th birthday like she had. There were other classmates that were just as, or almost as popular as she was, but she didn't associate with them. She didn't like sharing the spotlight. Anyway, they had their entourage and she had hers. She was a little obnoxious and hard to take at times, reminding us over and over again that she could have any boy at school. You'd think that someone like her, the center of everyone's attention, would date maybe the quarterback of the football team or the richest boy in school. But no, she dated boys that she could intimidate or that worshiped her.

Whoever she dated, she never hid the fact that she had more money, more status, or was better-looking. She had a better class of friends, and made it plain that her courting partner was lucky to be dating her, because they were below her standards. The last victim she dated was in our senior year. This young man was a person of few words. But when he did speak, the words were profound and grand--words for thought. He could hold his own. He was a member of the debate club and was a volunteer in the yearbook club. That was where they met. I could see what attracted her- he didn't wear designer brand clothes, come from a wealthy family, wasn't popular and didn't have a car. However, his personality was strong and well defined, which was one thing that she had never dealt with in anyone she dated in the past. But he did fit the profile of all the others, when it came to background and class status. So she took for granted that he was in awe of her, because she had things and popularity, or because many others would like to be in his place. But not him! You had to dig deeper to the bone to see all that his core was about. He was a young man with a plan, vision, and most of all, self-confidence. She disrespected him and took for granted that he would take the lack of respect. He dumped her! She was stunned, confused, and humiliated.

This type of rejection happens everyday to people who judge others from the outside, in. Has this ever happened to you?

"They have some nerve." Right! You were doing them a favor by allowing them to date you. You told your friends "They'll be back." Denial! "Its not like they'll be able to find someone like me." (Why would they want too?) You thought you were the cream of the crop, the top of the league, the best of the best. "They'll be back and when they come back, I'm gonna make sure they grovel." Still in denial! A week later, after you pick your face up off the floor, you changed your thinking, from "They'll be back," to "Do you think they are coming back?" Perplexed! You thought they would surely have come to their senses by now. Now you add a touch of criticism to help bolster the belief that you still have the upper hand.

A few more days go by. You have something to say. You've gone over the situation in your mind and pick up the phone to call them, because you would like them to know that there are no hard feelings. You also want them to know that you think the separation is for the best, but you just didn't know how to end things. Of course you have to protect your ego, but you never get the opportunity to make the grand gesture, because when you call, the number has been changed to an unpublished one. Anger!

You spend a lot of time wondering what happened, what did you do? Why did this person leave in that manner? A person's perception of himself or herself is much more intense, with a narrower view than the way others see them. Someone outside of you, sees the entire person who you are, what you do, and how you treat others.

The way someone is...their kindness, sincerity, honesty, and loyalty...these things are inside. I call this beauty, and those attributes are more than skin deep. This is really what we should be instilling in our children, and seeking in others, especially our mates or spouses.

Chapter 21

Why Do You Gamble On Love?

You don't have to be in Las Vegas to find a crap game with high stakes, because with relationships... the stakes are high. If we know the possible result of being in love is physical or mental suffering and distress, why do we search so hard to find it? Because, when we find love, what we get from it compares to nothing else.

Welcome positive energy into your life. When you step into an elevator, talk to the person who is in that "ship" with you for the moment. Don't just stand there. Open up your mouth and start facing your fears of communication. Let go of the past, to be ready for the future. If you go into a new courtship fearing it will fail, then there should be no surprise if it does. But if you go into the relationship as a confident person, expecting it to work out, there's no need to fear the outcome. Don't miss out on the possibility of finding happiness.

The feeling of newness— in experiences, conversations, and emotions, is so good that sometimes the feeling can heal, remove sorrow or take away pain. But on the same note, when experiences are bad, the pain caused from disappointment hurts like nothing else. Knowing all this, we are still willing to gamble on the odds of finding love that is good. You may not consider yourself a gambler because you don't go to casinos, but when it comes down to *real love* are you willing to gamble for the right jackpot? All relationships are a gamble. The differences between them are that some pay-off and others don't. Some have astronomically low odds, like a million to one, yet some have very high odds as good as a 99% chance of survival. The question is "Which type of relationships do you prefer to take your chances with?" In casinos, big payoffs are always accompanied by games with very low odds of winning. However, in relationships, the payoffs are the same with low odds and high odds, because the ultimate objective is to have a lasting relationship.

So how do I define high odds or low odds relationships? High odds relationships are ones where both participants took the time to intimately communicate their wants and their needs. "Low odds" or no D.I.C. relationships, are ones where the participants jump into being together, allowing their physical and financial assets to become involved before they ever really get to know each other. Only a few out of a million relationships may ever work out, and the chances of heartbreak are incredibly high.

Pain that comes from a broken heart cannot be fixed by having surgery. Healing takes your mind, to will the heartache away. Even with willpower, sometimes the hurt leaves scars so deep they may never disappear. Camouflaged only by a thin scab, these types of scars are responsible for creating most of the shallow people we meet. They have allowed themselves to become afraid of real love.

Part III: How You Like *You* Now?

Come on... don't fear love, embrace it! Learn from and build on it. You have the materials, now find someone that has the right mixture of glue to make it stick. Don't keep trying love the same way and expecting a different result. That's called *Crazy*! You control the pace for love, don't let love control you. Along the way, there are many rewards, ceremonies, and celebrations, but also repercussions, punishments, and the promise of The Good Book that you reap what you sow. Sometimes you will be the student, professor, or philosopher. I It doesn't matter what hat you are wearing, in the end the result is still the same. If you don't do your homework, you might learn your lessons the hard way.

How we feel about ourselves, generally lets us know if we are going to pass or fail.

Take some personal time out, to become certain what makes you, *you* and only you. Why do you know yourself? Why do you love yourself? And why do you deserve what you believe you deserve, for yourself? Do you know your self-worth? Don't deny your happiness. Loneliness can cause you sorrow, but when you use the power of your mind you know that you are never alone. You may get lonely, but the power of your mind will allow you to find that place within you that gives comfort, as well as company. You can have companionship in your life and still be lonely. If you are only happy when you are in a relationship, then you will keep finding temporary satisfaction. You are *you* for a reason, not by mistake. A higher power (that was out of your control) chose you, to *be* you. So take the time to find out why you are who you are, and what makes you, who you are. Always remember, you are perfect at being *you.*

When you give people the power to control what makes you the person you are, you're giving them permission to make "you", what they want you to be. Don't give away your power. They have their power and you have yours. You can only be *you,* one hundred percent of the time. You can't be anyone else, or vice versa. Spend time getting to know yourself, so that you may achieve the goal you're trying to reach. Let go of everything that is unhealthy, not encouraging, and destructive.

Part III: How You Like *You* Now?

Allow love to find you. Look inside your spirit and become its friend. Life is full of experiences. You can achieve the type of relationship you want, with good D.I.C. and with a simple child-like belief that you can have anything you want. Because of the mere fact that a child doesn't understand he "can't have", he believes he can. Believe that you won't get hurt in the next relationship. Love isn't harmful, destructive or painful. It's warm, friendly, loyal, honest, healthy, good and kind. If you believe you deserve good pay for good work, then surely you must believe you deserve good love for good love. Like The Good Book says, "you reap what you sow".

Some people live by the precept of "Don't ask, because they won't tell." I was in a relationship for five years, when I found out that he had gotten married. He'd been married for two months, when I heard about it. Once confronted, he said that he'd made a mistake and was going to annul the marriage. I remained in the relationship, even after the birth of a son within his first year of marriage. I was so convinced of his love for me, that I stayed with him for three more years. You may be reading

184

this and thinking this story is a mirror image of your life today. Believing, or rather wanting to believe, that if you gamble and wait faithfully on a lover, you will certainly win their heart. Well maybe, maybe not!

I believe most men will lie when the truth will do. Back then, I chose to believe that this meant he lied to everyone else, but not to me. I found out that he lied to everyone, about everything. I left the relationship with this lesson: what you see, is what you get - if it walks like a duck and quacks like a duck then it's a duck. The same is true in my scenario. If he lied when the truth would do, to other people he said that he cares about, then he would lie to me.

As in most relationships, everything about this one was shown to me before the end. I choose to ignore the clues. He would say one thing and mean another- I mean exactly what I say. He didn't know me well enough, to know that what I said I meant. I was familiar with him but didn't want to pay close enough attention, or I would have realized I didn't really know him. The differences in the way we communicated and our lack of compatibility in intimacy, affected the relationship. I take ownership of my decision to stay in a dead-end relationship, even though the truth was in front of me. Clearly, I was in denial. I gambled...and I crapped out.

Find love that wants to be found. Look for the love that is seeking you. Want the love that wants to love you back. Until you are ready and the other person is ready, until you both are satisfied completely with yourselves, you won't be able to find that perfect love. Don't look at what others have, be satisfied in knowing that in you there is perfect love and that is a 100% advantage.

Part IV:

Maybe -- Maybe Not!

Chapter 22

Friends Only Club

If you think you can remain in a platonic friendship with someone, when you know his preference is to have a romantic, intimate relationship with you, then you're facing a difficult challenge. Maybe not today, you don't feel any intimate attraction toward him, but that doesn't mean it won't happen. Still, you want to remain friends.

His goal is to convince you without being too forward or outwardly pushy, that he is the one you should be with. He moves on every hint of your wants and effortlessly eliminates your needs. And you're still holding out for friendship status.

Part IV: Maybe, Maybe Not!

It is very difficult to be friends with someone, when they make it clear in the beginning that you hold a physical attraction for them. You can say it won't go any further, but wait-- it's the right time. He makes your wants now haves, and needs no longer need. On this day the temperature was savagely hot. Because of the sweat and heat from your body, comfort is in wearing as close to nothing as possible. Your "I only want to be friends" friend, is mowing the grass. Through the screen from your back porch you see his shorts sticking to well-developed thighs that you hadn't noticed before.   You bring him a pitcher of cold water with crushed ice, and notice the front of his shorts are wet with sweat from the top, all the way down to his crotch, leaving very little to the imagination. As you stand there, he lifts the water to his lips and closes his eyes as if to enjoy every drop. You take a slow look at the way the muscles flex on your "I only want to be friends" friend, and then spot a tattoo on his right bicep. Guess what? As you dry his back off with a towel that you got off the clothesline, you touch him in a way that's not like a friend and say you find tattoos so-o-o-o sexy on a man.

OK! It can happen. Even I have been guilty of saying no, and with the right temptation, sometimes after an exhausting struggle, the no became yes.

If you are interested in only a friendship, make it clear by avoiding those intimate moments with that person, so you won't give any crossed signals. We are sexual beings. Sometimes there are just things in us, on certain days, certain moments, certain situations in our lives that trigger attractions we've never felt before. It is up to us, how we respond to the feelings. It's still just a thought, if we never act on it. Once we act on it, it is no longer in our heads.

There are some people we meet in our lives, who we know immediately (by sight, interest, conversation...etc.) will never be more than friends to us. Unlike certain other people, much to our surprise, for whom we immediately feel an attraction to become *more* than friends. Most of the time, something inside tells us this can only be a platonic friendship.

If the relationship begins with intentions of being more than friends and undergoes a change, be honest and convey your feelings if you want to remain just friends.

Not being honest when you only want to be platonic friends with someone who is interested in more, is wrong. It may not be easy, and he may not like what you say at the time, but you will respect yourself for being truthful. There are numerous relationships that started out as platonic, and developed into more. Often, being non-physical helped the start of successful, long-lasting romantic relationships. No pressure, no strain, no preconceived notion that this should be anything other than friendship. Sometimes, no physical contact when there is an initial attraction, is hard to comply with.

Co-workers that end up in relationships, have some of the most successful relationships because there is an initial intimacy. When people come together for a common interest like sports, church, or work and are unconnected sexually, they can be more comfortable being themselves. If everyone in the world looked the same, and communication was what we relied on to distinguish ourselves apart, we could all wear blinders and use our ears to hear who we are interested in having a friendship with. The problem is, we are *not* all the same and we don't wear blinders. But in "approaching" a relationship we should put on our blinders and depend on our D.I.C. skills and the knowledge that what sounds good and feels good, *is* good for us. That's why some friendship-based relationships last longer than purely romantic relationships. Are you blind to what they look like, and listen to what they sound like?

When I was younger, I told my mother that for me it's not important to talk with my relatives frequently, or to say "I love you" when I don't. What's important to me, is that I know who they are and accept them as a relative. I don't have to like or love them, just because we are related. I didn't choose them as a relative.

Her way of thinking was different. She was taught, as most of us are, (not by choice but by force) that you like and love your relatives, just because they are family. What we learn about trusting our feelings, and expressing affection as a child, prepares us for understanding life as an adult. This is how we learn to accept forced love. The way we (show or accept) love, has a lot to do with our childhood. Think back in your childhood, to when you were too young to know what love meant. Did you like or love all of your relatives? Did your parents tell you that you *must* love them because they were family?

What some children learn very early about the word "love", is that when they say it, they get something in return— a hug, kiss or a smile. Sometimes "I love you" is said as a bargaining tool to get things. Reality is, that when we're grown up and in a relationship, saying "I Love You" doesn't always feel warm, safe or guarantees us hugs. Because of what we learned as children, we stay in a relationship and try to force love.

Of course liking each and every one of our relatives would be nice, but if we don't, there is nothing wrong with that. I believe that it's important to allow a child to express when they love someone and when they don't. These are children, and much like some adults, their emotions will change from time to time. Help them to trust in themselves. Give them the freedom to know when love feels healthy, what feels right, and teach them to express their feelings and emotions.

When children are told that it's wrong not to love their parents, siblings or relatives, it sends out mixed signals. Maybe that is what causes us as adults, to be confused about relationships that are supposed to be love, but don't feel good or right. We try to force the love anyway.

When I got older, I told my mother that I was in full control of my emotions and I was aware of who I like and don't like, love and don't love. The fact that I did not love everyone, took my mother a while to understand, but now she accepts my right to choose.

In some ways, experiencing different kinds of love is like going back to childhood and starting all over, learning how to love in a way that is healthy for me. I am following my direction and trusting in my spirit to know what makes me happy, whom I am happy with, and whom I feel that I love. It's important that my mother validates what's good love to her, but more important that she allows me to do the same. We have a very good friendship and a loving relationship.

Part IV: Maybe, Maybe Not!

No matter how some people feel about you, how they try and force you to love them the way they are convinced that you should, you know within yourself, that he or she will always be a member of the Friends Only Club. This is OK. At least you have a good friend.

There was this wonderful man in my life for years. He was kind, gentle and vulnerable. Incarcerated for years in boarding schools, he spoke four languages fluently. Without a doubt, he would have made Peoples Magazine's 50 most beautiful people. One could compare his body to Adonis, the Greek God. He came from a good family, had an impeccable wardrobe, and sported a brilliant smile. The only thing he didn't have was the shining armor to go with his white horse. Yes, he had the white horse. Not just one, but a stable full. His family owns numerous blue ribbon horses, along with three vineyards on the west coast-- money was not a worry for him. Fortunately for me, his most important asset was his love – his love for me. He was always there for me, his family, and others. He took away my wants and filled all of my needs. He used to say, if I had a need that he could help me with, then I would no longer have that need. His want was far more unpredictable and as far as his needs being fulfilled, they relied on the cooperation of his want...and that was me.

He was generous with his money - not because he had so much, but because he could be. He gave thousands to health research organizations, as well as educational and charitable foundations. But his passion was equal rights. He used to say, "Act first. Believe you have the right, until someone says you don't, then act to prove you do." He was very giving with me. He paid for clothes I wanted, La Perla and Lise Charmel lingerie, jewelry he wanted me to have and trips I took with others. I always brought him back a souvenir, usually tourist stuff, a t-shirt, mug, or something trendy.

We met at a charity event for children in Northern Virginia. His mother was the Mistress of Ceremonies. It took place on a warm July day, and was held outside. The men wore navy jackets, white pants and starched shirts- some with ascots and some without. The women were in floral dresses -- strapless, criss-cross or spaghetti straps with tiny jackets to match. Their legs were bare with high heel strappy sandals, mostly Jimmy Choo, Manolo Blahnik and Gucci. The event reminded me of a scene from "Pretty Woman", with Richard Gere and Julia Roberts, where they were attending a polo match.

He was adopted. His parents were an older couple, mother 41 and father 45, when they adopted him at eight weeks old. They never had children of their own - for what reason, I don't know. He attended an Ivy League college where he completed his undergrad and grad, receiving his masters in Petroleum Engineering in four years, and Departmental Honors for the highest grade point average.

I couldn't tell that he was not their biological child, although for the first 15 minutes or so after meeting him, you might have a vague sense that something was not adding up. His father is of Persian decent and his mother Japanese. There was no mistaking that there was African-American in his bloodline because of his flawless caramel colored skin, round nose and full lips, but his eyes were true blue. Once you get over that initial surprise at the mosaic of ethnicity, you couldn't help but see the beauty in this rainbow family.

We met by mere coincidence. I was a volunteer, whose job it was to seat guests as they arrived at the event. It was scheduled to last for only four hours, but I had to be there an hour beforehand, to greet early arrivals. The gala was nearing its final hour and my feet were hurting. People were coming in and going out and my job was to seat them each time they came in. I was starting to feel a little fatigued and was not as organized as I had been at the start. The guests were changing seats throughout the event to sit near friends. So near the end, it was difficult to determine which seats were, and were not taken. Then a lovely older couple came in and I escorted them over to two empty seats at a table that appeared to be available. I was so pleased to find a clean table that seemed untouched, I didn't notice the handsome man standing to my right. "Thank you for coming," I said to the older couple. I turned left to go back to the door, when the handsome man grabbed my arm gently. I looked down in surprise when my arm stopped moving, while the rest of my body was going forward. The moment was exactly like the really great old romantic black and white movies when two lost lovers find each other again after fate has kept them apart.

He placed his finely manicured, yet masculine hands on my small curvy bicep. At that very moment, the aroma of sandalwood and citrus overwhelmed my senses. My legs weakened as I breathed in the familiar fragrance that could only have been a custom blend by Creed's Huile Parfumee. I was like a junkie getting the last bit of a fix. Wanting to see the face that came with this scent, my eyes began a delicious journey of mouth-watering, manly features. I hesitated...breathe... and moved inch-by-inch, thread-by-thread over his hand and on upwards. I stared at his wrist, banded by a Cartier watch and his French cuff shirt accented by a beautiful mother of pearl cuff link...breathe. Noticing next, the Italian Kiton blue wool suit that covered the remainder of his Brioni Egyptian shirt...breathe. Seeing the tightness in the jacket as my eyes moved slowly up his arm (breathe...breathe), he let go of my arm. My heart is beating fast (breathe...breathe) "Can I help you?" was all my mind could produce. I must have spoken too softly, so I repeated myself "Can I help you?"

"Yes, you can," he said. My thoughts exactly, I agreed silently. "Now that you have put someone in my seat, where would you like me to sit?"

"I'm sorry, I will be more than happy to move them."

"I was just kidding", he said as he introduced himself. "I can sit anywhere, just as long as everyone is having a good time. Don't you agree?" he asked. Oh, how I agreed! "Anyway, if I can't find a seat, I can always stand at the door with you, that way I will get close to a seat but never quite get to one" he said and smiled. It was such a... luscious smile, on top of the boyish charm and sparkling eyes. He stood about 6'5" tall, with large pretentious shoulders, and a small waist with long, long pant legs. (Come on, what did you expect... he had his clothes on and look at the title of the chapter.)

Our meeting was definitely a first sight attraction that quickly turned to lust. Our friendship lasted for five years. The first three, he spent unconditionally pursuing me. There was never any romance between us in the consummated sense. It is not that he didn't try romancing me. He did- many, many times with fine dining and lots of expensive gifts. He use to quote Proverbs 18:22, "the only thing that would have made him feel as if he has findeth a good thing is to have me as a wife."

I have felt less attraction or respect for some men in my past, and consummated the relationship anyway. The reason why I didn't... commit, to this fine man was because I didn't get that earth shattering feeling. You know, that something inside you that turns on the "Yes"... in your brain or other parts of your body. I was honest and I told him.

Regrets, I don't have, but I do wonder from time to time what wonderful woman he finally found. I hope he reads this book.

Chapter 23

Discipline of Intimacy and Communication

When someone new says that they love me, my answer is "to know me is to love me". Even though it may be a very flippant response, I sincerely mean that if you love me, then one is confident that you know me. Because I feel to know me *is* to love me. I am confident that if you truly know me, than I am worth loving. It doesn't necessarily mean that everyone who knows me would agree, but because of the love that I have for myself, my perspective of how I feel about myself, matters more. I have love enough to love myself. I'm very intimate with who I am. I'm happy with my decision to communicate and eliminate unnecessary worry and wonder.

You might have noticed by now, that I have not stressed the importance of finding love in your life. The need for love – love of others and self-love, is a fundamental necessity of life. Love gives us energy that adds to our contentment and longevity.

I enjoy attention and affection, most definitely. I'm seeking love that is respectful, trustworthy, warm, and sincere. When some people choose a mate, they require much less compatibility then when choosing a best friend. If you look at the elements that allow us to call someone a best friend, often times the root that makes friendships last, is that we truly like and/or admire the person.

Before you take a mate, take this test:

Answer questions (1-10) today.

1. What makes a friend a friend?

2. What is your interpretation of an associate?

3. Do you have a best friend? What makes that person a best friend?

4. How long has this person been your best friend?

5. What do you have in common with your best friend?

6. What do you admire most about your best friend?

7. Have you ever met your best friend's family? Do you interact with your family in the same way that your best friend does with theirs?

8. Have you ever met your best friend's other friends? Was there a sense of loyalty between your best friend and the other friends?

9. Have you ever met your best friend's co-workers? Would you say they respect each other?

10. Does your best friend live their life, similar to the way that you live yours?

When you meet someone you are considering as a mate, ask him to answer the same questions. Then compare the answers. If the relationship progresses into certainty, before you utter the word "love" you re-answer the questions, changing "best friend" to "mate". See how many of the questions you can answer, and if you are comfortable with your responses.

Once you utter the word "love", consider these questions that are rarely thought of in the beginning stages of a relationship:

1. Do you have confidence in your mate?

2. Do you make We, Us, and Ours a priority?

3. Do you get back what you give?

4. Would you choose your mate for a friend?

5. Do you admire your mate?

6. Do you support your mate's dreams?

7. Do you have the same spiritual beliefs?

8. Do you need your mate to feel complete?

9. Do you have the same sexual drive?

10. Do you share good D.I.C. with your mate?

Freedom Comes With Taking Ownership!

Write down your desires in a journal. Describe to yourself, what love feels like to you. Tell others what love does, and doesn't feel like to you. Remember, what you define as love may be different from how others feel. Respect others' characterization of what love feels like to them. Everyone's definition of love, is right for *them*. You just need to find someone whose definition is the same as yours.

Let go of any destructive communications in your life. Celebrate what's right with your relationship and as a "We", work on what's wrong. This is the technique of gaining good Discipline of Intimacy and Communication.

Communication & Intimacy Techniques:

When you see someone for the first time his look or demeanor piques an interest to get to know him. "Chatty Cathy" is not the way to go. Practice the art of small talk.

The art of small talk: how to converse easily with new acquaintances!

Part IV: Maybe -- Maybe Not!

Talk less... listen more. Make mental notes to learn more about a person's interests.

Say things like...so what do you think? What do you like? What would you do? This increases the chances of finding out more about these people.

Also, if you're not sure about the subject, listening gives you a basic idea of the topic, and hopefully you will feel more comfortable joining in.

Easy steps to untangle mixed signals and ensure crystal-clear two-way communication in a relationship.

Make it clear, what you want in a relationship.

Remember anything unconfirmed is assumed.

Phrase your question in a way to gain clarity: *So what I understand you to be saying is...?*

Look for body language that confirms you are being understood... nods, eye contact, etc.

Ask questions like... Are we in agreement?

I am looking for _____ in a relationship.

How you can make an unforgettable first impression in 2 minutes or less!

Smile

Eye to eye contact

Firm handshake, cup your left hand under both joined hands

Remember names

Appear confident

Untangling "mixed signals": Ways to send (and receive) crystal-clear communications.

Sending:

Just because you SPEAK doesn't mean you are being heard

Speak clearly and directly. Ask straightforward questions

Ask if they understand (look for acknowledgement)

Make your point clear

Receiving:

Ask questions that make it clear you need clarification

Remember if it's NOT confirmed, it's assumed

If you are not certain, get clarity by asking questions

When you've said something the wrong way or the wrong thing... how to recover and mend fences quickly.

Part IV: Maybe -- Maybe Not!

I apologize

Please, will you forgive me?

Remember a genuine apology never has a "BUT" behind it

A <u>SINCERE APOLOGY</u> is the best way to mend fences quickly

I apologize for raising my voice

I accept full responsibility

Poem

Why Do I Will Your Will?

I come to you and say, "I want to do this". You say, "No, do that". Your will be done.

Why do I will your will?

I come to you and say, "I'm going to do it tomorrow". You say "No, today". Your will be done.

Why do I will your will?

I come to you and say, "*This* is better for me." You say, "No, *that* is best". Your will be done.

Why do I will your will?

I come to you and say, "I don't feel good." You say, "No, you feel fine". Your will be done.

Why do I will your will?

I come to you and say, "I am ill." You say, "No, you're well". Your will be done.

Why do I will your will?
I died today.

I didn't know what to do.

I saw a stranger at the passageway of the Pearly Gates sitting on a throne.

I said to the stranger, I really wanted to do this, but he said, do that.

Part IV: Maybe -- Maybe Not!

I wanted to do it tomorrow, but he said do it today.

I thought *this* was better for me, but he said *that* was best.

I said, *I* don't feel good; he said *I* felt fine.

I knew I was ill, but he said I was well and so I died.

Now I'm here, alone with my own thoughts and will to be done.

So can you tell me what I should do?

The stranger looked at me and said, "Because I love you, thy will be done".

It was obvious that the stranger didn't know what I should do, or else he would have told me.

Then He spoke once more "*I am God* my child. Because of my love for you, I gave you your will. I stood at the door of your heart but never came in." "Why?" I asked.

God turned to me and said "My child you never willed me in." Because, I Love You, I Won't Will Your Will...your will was done.

Author,
Terry Smith

Chapter 24

My Prayer For You

There is no requirement nor will you wither away if you don't fall in love during your lifetime. The feelings that come with love are wonderful, but love is sometimes unexpressive and can be hurtful and permanently damaging. Everyone's journey in life is filled with expectations, disappointments, and possibilities, but few guarantees - that's the way life is. Having the discipline to develop a plan for your journey in life, will allow you to deal with those inevitable feelings of loneliness and emptiness. Developing that plan begins with determining your needs and identifying your wants. In the process, you will also develop the ability to rightly divide relationships that have good DIC and those that have bad DIC.

Ask all the questions that you need, to feel confident about your decision when you have to make a choice. A productive exchange of questions that enlightens and builds understanding is the only way to make certain you will be satisfied with the outcome. In Chapter 2: "What is Good D.I.C.," I discussed how many people are uncomfortable asking questions. Often, long after the conversation, we find ourselves wishing we had asked something that we chose to leave unspoken. With discipline and practice, you can ask questions in a way that reduces discomfort. Phrasing questions in a way that invites dialogue helps the receiver and you, too.

I heard you say, "I'm trying." So why is it that you're unhappy all the time? "I am trying to make him happy and it's making me miserable." *Teaching the D.I.C.* went through a number of different personal testimonies--the woman letting go of her emotions for a relationship ended by death, relationships meant to be platonic but with the right elements (scorching hot day, tight shorts and a sexy tattoo) changed to an intimate romance, and others. These stories offered inside, face-to-face, real life experience that allowed you to see yourself in their mirrors.

My prayer for you is that you are decisive and take charge of your will. Use the Discipline of Intimacy and Communication test with every close relationship in your life.

Now that we are at the end of this book, I hope you have become a person who can take ownership of the way you communicate. You made a choice. Maybe a bad choice, but the good thing about your choice, is- it was yours.

Understanding the accountability for your choices is not always as clear as knowing that walking in front of a moving car will get you hit, but it was your choice to take the risk. Many times, without life's unavoidable lessons—heartache, loss and maturity, you might never know that your choice is the only one that counts for your life.

Closing words to live by: Nothing in life is original. Every day is a repeat of something that has already happened to someone else. The difference is how they, and you go through it. Today is a good day! The sad thing about the past, is that some of our friends are not here with us in the present. The best thing about a new year, is the celebration of "new". The good thing about yesterdays, is the worry about them as tomorrows, is gone. The greatest thing about *today,* is right now. Never wait on tomorrows... they never come. I pray that you have good D.I.C. in your life.

Be Blessed...*(wink)*

To Attend <u>Teaching the D.I.C.</u> Workshops contact:

www.TerrySmithOnline.com

www.FirstPressDirect.com

First Press Direct, Inc.

2778 Cumberland Blvd., #233

Smyrna, GA 30080

Now You Are Ready To Make A Change!

Make a list from 1-10 of the things that you admire and respect about your mate or the top qualities you are looking for in a mate.

i.e.)   He makes an effort to spend quality time with me
i.e.)   Someone who considers my feelings

1.)

2.)

3.)

4.)

5.)

6.)

7.)

8.)

9.)

10.)

List Your Non-Negotiables!

List the things you don't like, and will not compromise on. "One" should be the most important quality your soul mate must have. Also make a note of what on the list you *are* willing to compromise on.

i.e.)   My preference is someone who does not drink alcohol (compromise – wine occasionally)

i.e.)   Someone who dates more then one person at a time (no compromise)

1.)

2.)

3.)

4.)

5.)

6.)

7.)

8.)

9.)

10.)

NOTES:

To Find Out More About The Author's next book entitled:

Men Will Lie
When the Truth
Will Do

The King, His Queen and the Other Woman

Preview the first chapter at: www.TerrySmithOnline.com

First Press Direct, Inc.
2778 Cumberland Blvd., #233
Smyrna, GA 30080

NEED HELP GETTING YOUR BOOK EDITED, MARKETED AND PUBLISHED?

First Press Direct, Inc.

Is seeking new or first time published authors.

First Press Direct
2778 Cumberland Blvd., #233
Smyrna, GA 30080

www.FirstPressDirect.com

NOTES:

NOTES:

NOTES:

NOTES:

ABOUT THE AUTHOR

Upon catching the reader's attention with the book's bold, brow-raising title, Smith looks forward to garnering a mixed readership, inclusive of both men and women whom are enjoying new or long-term relationships, between relationships and even those whom are nursing their wounds as the result of a broken bond. "After reading the book, I hope that my audience will understand that we are all deserving of the freedom to communicate our needs. By doing so, we can ultimately open the door to owning our choices."

When asked to give voice to the primary source of her own frustration when interacting with a prospective partner, Smith states simply, "Deception. I do everything in my power *not* to ask for a second chance, therefore, I find it very difficult to deal with folks who say one thing and do another," she says. "Many people live their lives with the false expectation that they will *always* have a second chance, which is both self-serving and unrealistic." Point well taken...

In addition to her current book project, Smith plans to take her message on the road. Aptly entitled, "Good D.I.C.," the national seminars will feature her own brand of hands-on instruction and also provide a forum for open discussion among participants. With the publication of *Teaching the D.I.C.* to her credit, Smith is currently at work on her first fiction book, *Men Will Lie When The Truth Will Do*, which will be published by First Press Direct, Inc. during 2003.

Author's Photograph

db Dexter Browne – Photographer
Adam Christopher - Makeup Artist
Terrell Simon - Hair Stylist